CHRISTIAN MISSION
IN A PLURALISTIC WORLD

John Patrick Brennan

CHRISTIAN MISSION IN A PLURALISTIC WORLD

 St Paul Publications

Cover: photo by L. Lees

St Paul Publications
Middlegreen, Slough SL3 6BT, England

Copyright © St Paul Publications 1990

ISBN 085439 326 9

Typeset by Grove Graphics, Tring
Printed by Dotesios Printers Ltd, Trowbridge, Wiltshire

St Paul Publications is an activity of the priests and brothers of the Society of St Paul who proclaim the Gospel through the media of social communication

TO MY PARENTS
JOHN AND KATHLEEN BRENNAN

Ackowledgments

Grateful acknowledgment is hereby given to:

Missio, Aachen, West Germany, for its partial funding of a one-year study-leave which made the writing of this book possible. Likewise I would like to express my thanks to the Director of Missionswissenschaftliches Institut, St Augustin, near Bonn, for the warm hospitality extended to me there, the valuable advice received, and the excellent library facilities placed at my disposal.

The following publishers for the permission to quote copyright material for this publication:

Burns & Oates for *Catholicism* by Henri de Lubac, London 1950; *God's Rule and Kingdom* by R. Schnackenburg, London 1963.

Cambridge University Press for *The Incarnation* by Brian Hebblethwaite, Cambridge 1987.

Geoffrey Chapman for *The Mystery of the Church* by Yves Congar, London 1965.

Collins for *On being a Christian* by Hans Küng, London 1975.

Columbia University Press for *Christianity and the Encounter of the World Religions* by Paul Tillich, New York 1963.

Darton Longman & Todd for *Theological Investigations* vol XXI by Karl Rahner, London 1988.

Dominican Publications for *Documents of Vatican II* by Austin Flannery OP (ed.), Dublin 1975.

E.J. Dwyer Publications for *Christian Hope and the Liberation of Man* by Juan Alfaro, Rome 1976.

Edinburgh Press House for *The Christian Message in a non-Christian World* by Hendrik Kraemer, Edinburgh 1938.

Les Éditions du Cerf for *L'Église de Vatican II* by G. Baraúna, Paris 1967.

Gregorian University Publications, for "Evangelization, Dialogue and Development" by M. Dhavamony (ed.), in *Documenta Missionalia* 5, 1972, pp. 135.157.358, Rome 1972.

Helicon Press for *The Wide World My Parish* by Yves Congar, Baltimore 1961.

Herder & Herder for *Christ in the Theology of St Paul* by Lucien Cerfaux, New York 1959.

Institute of Theological Reflection for "The Kingdom of God and World Religions" in *Vidyajyoti* 51 (November 1987) by Jacques Dupuis, Delhi 1987.

Liguori Publications for *The Sacraments and Your Everyday Life* by Bernard Häring, Missouri 1976.

Orbis Books for *God's Chosen People* by Walter Bühlmann, Maryknoll 1978; *Christian Faith in a Religiously Plural World* by D. Dawe and J. B. Carmen (eds), Maryknoll 1978; *Christians and Religious Pluralism* by A. Race, Maryknoll 1982; *No Other Name? a critical survey of Christian attitudes towards world religions* by Paul Knitter, Maryknoll 1985.

Paulist Press for *The Intra-Religious Dialogue* by Raymond Panikkar, New York 1978.

Revue Internationale de Théologie for "Who belongs to the Church?" by Boniface Willems in *Concilium* 1/1965, p. 70 (Burns & Oates, London); "Catholic Theology of Religions at a Crossroads" by Paul Knitter in *Concilium* 1/1986, p. 103 (T&T Clark, Edinburgh).

SCM Press for *Christ: The Christian Experience in the Modern World* by E. Schillebeeckx, London 1980; *The Apostles' Creed in the Light of Today's Questions* by Wolfhart Pannenberg, London 1972.

The Seabury Press for *Concise Sacramentum Mundi* by Karl Rahner (ed.), New York 1975.

Sheed & Ward for *The Church* by Hans Küng, London 1967; *Revelation and Theology* I by E. Schillebeeckx, London 1987 edition; *World and Church* by E. Schillebeeckx, London 1971.

SPCK for *Elucidations* by Hans-Urs von Balthasar, London 1975.

Theology Digest for "The Church as Sacrament" by Gustave Martelet SJ in *Theology Digest* vol 22/1 1974, St Louis.

Veritas Publications for *The Reality of Jesus* by Dermot A. Lane, Dublin 1975.

Westminster Press for *God has Many Names* by John Hick, Philadelphia 1980.

World Council of Churches for "Urgent Need of a Common Mission" by Metropolitan Emilianos in *International Review of Mission* vol LXXXII, no. 286, April 1983, Geneva; "Christianity in a Pluralistic World. The Economy of the Holy Spirit" by Mgr Georges Khodr in *The Ecumenical Review* vol XXIII/2, 1971, Geneva.

Contents

1

The problem

What is the relationship of Christianity to other religions? Should Christianity continue to proclaim her message to people of other faiths? Is salvation to be found in the other religions as such? Is conversion any longer to be the goal of mission? How are adherents of other religions to be saved if they explicitly reject the proclamation of the Gospel? These are some of the questions being asked today within the Christian Church. They are questions which the Church cannot avoid asking, and to which she must strive to give answers. The German theologian, Walter Kasper, writing on the question "Are Non-Christian religions salvific?" said: "Indeed it is with this question and the response that is given to it that the meaning and position of the Church in history stands or falls."[1] Archbishop Lourdusamy, the former Secretary of the Congregation for the Evangelization of Peoples (*Propaganda*) has said that the "encounter with world religions appears to be one of the signs of the time which no theologian or Church can ignore with impunity."[2] Harold Coward calls it "one of the key issues in Christian self-understanding."[3] Such quotations can easily be multiplied.

This problem is one that affects the Church in every fibre of her being and activity. It poses profound questions for her understanding of Christ, of the Incarnation, of her own nature, what she means by faith, revelation and salvation and how she defines these in relation to the faith, revelation and salvation claimed by other religions. It poses practical questions. How does one draw up a syllabus of Religious Education that will be acceptable to all in a multi-religious community or society? To what extent can the Church really enter into a true dialogue with people of other faiths? Indeed, the answer we give to the question of our relationship with other religions will depend on, and in a certain measure form, our understanding of the Church and of our very own being as Christians. Because of the intimate social nature of our human constitution we cannot adequately understand ourselves without understanding our relationship with others.

To sum up the whole question as succinctly as possible we ask: to what extent is Jesus Lord? How are we to understand the universal significance of Jesus Christ? And, as so often in the history of the Church and of her theology, it is in the area of her mission that the problem of her relationship with other religions is experienced in its most acute form. The Second Vatican Council has told us that the Church is, of her very nature, missionary. But the question is, *how* is she to be missionary in a pluralistically religious world? How do we proclaim the uniqueness of Jesus Christ, his Lordship, in the face of similar claims from the followers of other religions? How do we harmonize the fact of the universal call to salvation alongside the scandalous particularity of Jesus Christ? Are we to be insensitive, triumphalistic or downright domineering and dismissive of the claims of others? What, for example, is our response when our Muslim brothers say that God has spoken his definitive and perfect Word in the Holy Qu'ran? How are we to account for the salvation of the four-fifths of humanity who do not know of Christ or, at least, do not accept him as their Saviour? How are we to reconcile our faith in the fact that God in Jesus Christ has brought about the salvation of all humanity and at the same time recognize that such a claim is rejected by the vast majority of the human race? How are we to believe in a good, caring and all-powerful God and Father when the greater proportion of our brothers and sisters do not know of this love and care?

These questions are not new and are in fact as old as Christianity itself. What is new is the urgency with which they seek answers. And unfortunately it is sad but true that the vast majority of our Christians are ill-equipped to attempt an answer. Many attempts have been made at solving the problem (and we will look at some of them in the course of this chapter) but it must be said here at the very start that so far no universally acceptable solution has been found. Perhaps there is no solution and we must say that it forms part of the mystery of God's plan. However, even if this were the case, we are still not dispensed from the efforts to seek an understanding of the faith that we profess. As the Irish theologian, R. P. C. Hanson, remarked some years ago, "Religion protected by piety from critical investigation becomes fantasy."[4] "Always be prepared to make a defence to anyone who calls you to account for the hope that is in you" (1 Pet 3:15). A Christian theology that is at all worthy of the name must give an unreserved welcome to the questions of the present day.

The reasons why the problem has become so pressing in modern times are manifold. We live in a world characterized by profound and rapid change. It is generally admitted that the world has seen more changes in the past fifty years than it witnessed in the preceding five hundred. The twentieth century is one marked by enormously increased mobility. Mass movements of peoples, in search of work, fleeing from war or other problems, the internationalization of studies, etc., all have contributed to creating in the Western World at least a truly cosmopolitan environment. In the so-called First World mass tourism has opened up all five continents to the ordinary person as never before. Where formerly other religions were, by and large, confined to certain geographical areas of the globe, and therefore did not really impinge on the lives of the vastmajority of Christians – apart from the relatively few such as professional mis- sionaries, sailors, merchants and the like – today they have become a very visible and increasingly audible aspect of everyday life in our cities. They have become in a real, existential sense *world* religions. One hour at the inter- national airports of Heathrow or Schiphol is enough to con- vince one of this. Mosques and temples of all sorts are to be found alongside the churches and synagogues of our European cities.

This presence is further emphasized and underlined by

the mass media. Nightly, on our television screens, the reality is brought home to us that Christianity is but one way of understanding and honouring the divinity and that millions of people throughout the world have other ways. Never before has so much information been available as regards the ways in which the different peoples of the world live and think. The problems of the Sunni and Shi'ite Muslims are presented and discussed. The infinite variety of Hindu life and forms, the monastic routine of Tibetan monks, the Zen form of meditation, the Japanese styles of prayer are all popular subjects of innumerable discussion panels and chat-shows. In this way the extraordinary variety of religions to be found in our ever shrinking world forms part of the mental background of the men and women of the West. The reality of the Global Village (or, perhaps more accurately, the Global City) has its repercussions on our Christian faith and how we respond to it.

Another aspect of our contemporary world is the ever-greater and deeper historical consciousness. Humanity has existed on earth for many thousands of centuries – Christianity only for the past twenty of these. In terms of the age of humanity Christianity is but an infant. As moderns we are increasingly aware of our historical nature and the extent to which we are conditioned by it. Arising from this there is a growing disquiet in the face of all claims of religious and cultural absolutes. This consciousness of relativeness is particularly strong among the young, who feel that all absolute claims are not only arrogant and unjust but also that they are unsubstantiated. Furthermore, due to this historical nature of our being they can never be substantiated. They ask: can any merely historical reality be absolute, valid for all times, past, present and future, and for all peoples? Despite what would seem to be an innate tendency towards ethnocentrism, there is a certain wariness against all attempts to constitute one's own culture, or one's own religion, as being normative for all mankind. In any dialogue with the modern world, whether one is in agreement with these factors or not, they must be taken into account.

Again, yet another phenomenon of recent years – and one that has relevance to our theme – is the growing missionary thrust of other world religions. The modern missionary aggressivity of Islam (as seen by many Western eyes!) is well known and does not have to be underlined for anyone working in West Africa today. We have also seen the emergence of other religions vying for adherents on the streets of our European cities, whether it be the proponents of Zen meditation, the dedicated followers of Haré Khrishná or the disciples of Brother Moon. The followers of these religions are demanding, as their right, equal time and opportunity on the public mass media in order to proclaim and celebrate their faiths. Likewise they are demanding, as in England and West Germany, to have the teaching of their faiths imparted to their children in the state schools. All around us we see evidence of the fact that each nation and ethnic group struggles for survival, fights to maintain its own identity and its right to exist. In the traditional Christian mission fields this struggle is closely related to the reaction against colonialism, even though political independence has been achieved in practically all cases. Many thinking people are conscious of the fact that very often this independence is far from complete and the presence of the Christian missionary not infrequently represents for such people this incompleteness of their independence. The legitimate desire to achieve full independence – economic, cultural, technical, educational and religious, as well as political – helps to explain the opposition to Christian missionaries from abroad which is sometimes found, particularly among the better educated. Yet, on the other hand, it must be recognized that today all nations – and indeed all religions – are interdependent, and the destiny of one can have, and does have, repercussions on all. More than ever before we are becoming conscious that we are our brothers' keepers.

Coupled with this, we must also recognize the fact that over the past quarter of a century there has been a marked decline in the Christian commitment to mission, at least on the part of the Christian Church of the West. In this area we find a growing sense of confusion regarding the rightness of mission. Some have even gone so far as to claim that for the good of the young Churches a moratorium on mission should be declared in these countries.[5] Others ask the question: mission, yes, but how? What methods are appropriate for today's world? Are we to continue to try and convert people anymore? Is dialogue the new name of missionary activity?

All the above reasons have contributed in varying degrees to creating the situation we have today vis-à-vis world religions and their relationship to Christianity.

Before I go on to outline some of the positions that have been taken up on this question, a few words would not perhaps be out of place regarding what we mean by religion.

"Religion" is one of those words which in recent years has fallen into discredit (although admittedly this is a purely Western phenomenon and it can be argued that it is only in the West that it could become a problem).[6] Some would claim that religion as such is a mere abstraction and does not correspond to any given reality. It is true that the term religion is notoriously difficult to define. Even the etymology of the word is in dispute. Does it come from the Latin *religare*, or *religere* or *relegere*? From what standpoint are we to define the term? Sociological? Psychological? Historical? Philosophical? Theological? It is obvious that the standpoint would have enormous consequences for the resultant "definition". Moreover, it must not be forgotten that each one of us is profoundly conditioned by our own individual life experiences. By the very fact that we have been born into a specific context, been brought up in a specific religion – in our case, Christianity – or a specific religious environment, our way of looking at religion, of understanding it, is deeply influenced.

However, for the sake of this present work, religion will be understood as a specific response given on the part of a definite community to an experience of the transcendent and expresses itself in a definite form of rites, worship and in a certain ethical orientation. Some might prefer to describe it as a response given by a specific group to the questions regarding the existence, being and activity of the human person in the world. The different religions are thus understood as the various responses to humanity's questions regarding meaning. Here we will not go into the question of whether religions are purely man-made, or whether Christianity as such is a religion at all. Insofar as it is a response to the transcendent God, it is a religion and can, I think, be rightly regarded as such.

We now come to the different responses that have been given in modern times to the problem of the relationship of Christianity to other religions. Here I will merely present them and refer the reader to the places where they are more extensively elaborated. I will present them under the headings of the three different approaches which by now have become almost traditional. These are the exclusivistic approach, the inclusivistic approach, and the pluralist approach. In doing so I am perfectly aware of the danger of injustice being done to specific theologians in such a treatment. In trying to be concise and synthetic one inevitably runs the risk of overlooking the nuances of the individual theologians in the presentation of their views, and therefore a sketchy outline of a specific position rather than being a faithful reproduction may end up as a caricature. But sometimes caricatures, with their emphasis on a salient feature, can help to clarify a basic understanding of the subject in question.

Exclusivism

I term that approach Exclusivistic which holds that outside Christianity there is no salvation. This view is based on the conviction that Jesus Christ is the sole criterion by which all religions are to be judged. Such a view is generally found today among the members of the Evangelical Churches, but until recent times it was more or less the traditional view of the majority of Roman Catholics. Indeed, I think it is not untrue to say that it is the view with which the greater number of present-day Catholics grew up. Its biblical basis (although in this whole question it is a particularly hazardous venture to base one's claim on specific biblical texts) is to be found in such verses as "I am the way, and the truth, and the life; no one comes to the Father, but by me" (Jn 14:6). "And there is salvation in no one else, for there is no other name under heaven given among men by which we must be saved" (Acts 4:12).

In the tradition of the Church the position is also very strong and the oft-quoted sentence of Origen is invariably brought out in relation to it: "Extra ecclesiam nemo salvatur" – "Outside the Church no one is saved".[7] Cyprian has the same idea: "There is no salvation outside the Church".[8] Likewise there are many statements of the Magisterium: the Fourth Lateran Council (D. 802); Innocent III, Profession of Faith for Waldenses (D. 792); Boniface VIII, *Unam Sanctam* (D. 870-875); the Council of Florence, *Decree for the Jacobites* (D. 1351); Pius IX, *Singulari Quadam* (D. old ed. 1647), *Quanto Conficiamur Moerore* (D. 2866); Pius XII, *Humani Generis* (AAS 1950, p. 571), *Letter to Cardinal Cushing* (8-8-1949, D. 3866–3873). In the light of all this there can be no doubt that an exclusivistic understanding of the necessity of Christ and of his Church for salvation has been the traditional teaching of Catholicism even though since the Second Vatican Council it is no longer her formal teaching. The approach has sometimes been termed the ecclesiocentric approach.

A particularly powerful exposition of the exclusivistic approach is that set forth over fifty years ago by Hendrick Kraemer in preparation for the International Missionary Conference held at Tambaram in 1938. His main argument is that the event of Christ belongs to a totally different order of reality than that of other religions. For him, Christianity and other religions just simply cannot be compared. He writes:

> The *Christian Revelation* places itself over against the many efforts to apprehend the totality of existence. It asserts itself as the record of God's self-disclosing and recreating revelation in Jesus Christ, as an apprehension of existence that revolves around the poles of divine judgement and divine

salvation, giving the divine answer to this demonic and guilty disharmony of man and the world.[9]

It must be admitted that the Exclusivistic approach is very attractive. It proclaims clearly and unambiguously the central truth that Christianity is the one true religion, precisely because revelation and salvation are only offered to humanity in and through Jesus Christ. It is in line with what the Bible seems to proclaim clearly and what the main stream of Tradition has understood for well nigh two thousand years.[10] It has an undeniable inner logic. However, while granting all of this, it is a position that is severely criticized today for a number of reasons.

As regards the biblical basis of Exclusivism, it can be shown that there are other texts in the Bible which point in precisely the opposite direction and likewise within the Tradition of the Church — particularly in the early centuries — there is an important alternative stream which takes up a different position vis-à-vis the salvation of people outside the Church. It can be argued that this other stream is an equally valid interpretation of the facts of Scripture. We will see this when we look at the Inclusivistic approach.

Secondly, it can be alleged that the Exclusivistic position is completely arbitrary and is totally independent of any knowledge of other religions. As Raymond Panikkar has remarked, it "bears the intrinsic weakness of assuming an almost purely logical conception of truth and the uncritical attitude of an epistemological naïveté".[11] Among the Evangelicals in particular, the Exclusivistic approach would seem to rest on the conviction that Christianity is not a religion at all and can in no way be compared with other religions. Following Barth[12] they understand "religions" as being purely man-made and as such are totally incapable of being the bearers of eternal salvation. They are mere human attempts to give answers to questions of existence. Christianity, on the other hand, they would regard as being first and foremost a *faith* — that is, something God-given, a gift from the Divine, and precisely because it is such, it alone can save. Insofar as Christianity might be regarded as a religion, that is, insofar as it contains man-made elements, it is like all other religions and must submit itself to the critique of faith. For the Exclusivist, therefore, all other religions are *a priori* condemned as being incapable of providing salvation.

Finally, the Exclusivistic approach tends to bypass or neglect the second leg of Revelation in this whole question, namely, that God wills the salvation of all men without exception. In the light of their position and the actual historical reality of the world in which we live, where the vast majority of humanity do not in fact accept Christ or his Church, it is perhaps an aspect of Revelation they would rather leave buried in the mystery of God.

In practice, I think it can be fairly said that while we may find remnants of the Exclusivistic attitude it is hardly defended in the Catholic Church today, especially since Vatican II.

Inclusivism

By Inclusivism is meant the position or approach which holds that salvation is to be found in all religions but that this salvation is ultimately from and through Jesus Christ. Christ, it is claimed, is in some mysterious way present and active in all other religions. This approach aims at "holding together two equally binding convictions: the operation of God's grace in all the great religions of the world working for salvation and the uniqueness of the manifestation of that grace of God in Christ which makes a universal claim to be the final way of salvation".[13]

Biblically, this position would base itself primarily on Luke and Acts, which tend to emphasize the universal nature of Christ's saving activity. It calls attention to St Paul's going out to other religions and particularly to the Areopagus scene: "Men of Athens, I perceive that in every way you are very religious. For as I passed along, and observed the object of your worship, I also found an altar with this inscription, 'To an unknown God'. What therefore you worship as unknown, this I proclaim to you" (Acts 17:22–23).

Again, solid backing from among the Fathers can be produced for maintaining this position. For example, Justin wrote:

> We have been taught that Christ is the first-born of God, and we have declared that he is the Word of whom every race is partaker; and those who lived reasonably were Christians, even though they have been thought atheists; as among the Greeks, Socrates and Heraclitus, and men like them. And among the Barbarians, Abraham, Ananias, and Azarias and Misael and Elias, and many others whose actions and names we now decline to recount because it would be tedious.[14]

In Clement of Alexandria we find similar ideas:

> Wherefore also the Lord, drawing the commandments, both the first which he gave and the second, from one fountain, neither allowed those who were before the law to be without the law nor permitted those who were unacquainted with the principles of the Barbarian philosophy to be without restraint. For, having furnished the one with the commandments and the other with philosophy, he shut up unbelief to the Advent. Whence everyone who believes not is without excuse. For, by a different process of advancement, both Greeks and Barbarians, he leads to the perfection which is by faith. And if any of the Greeks passing over the preliminary training of the Hellenic philosophy, proceeds directly to the true teaching, he distances others, though an unlettered man, by choosing the compendious process of salvation by faith to perfection. Everything then which did not hinder a man's choice from being free, he made and rendered auxiliary to virtue, in order that there might be revealed somehow or other, even to those capable of seeing dimly, the only almighty, good God, from eternity to eternity, saving by his Son.[15]

Even though this line of reasoning tended to die out in the early Church — especially after the "conversion" of Constantine — it never completely disappeared and such ideas can be found in the mediaeval theologians such as Raymond Lull (c. 1233–c. 1315) and Nicholas of Cusa (1401–1464). Nicholas is particularly interesting. The shock occasioned by the fall of Constantinople to the Muslims in 1453 immediately brought home to him the problem of the relationship of the many different religions throughout the world to one another and to Christianity. In an openness of spirit and broad-mindedness, extraordinary for his time, he was willing to give each religion a hearing and tried to see how they integrated with the Christian faith in the uniqueness of salvation. In his work, *De Pace Fidei*, he presents a defence of the idea of salvation being found outside of Christianity pointing out how important aspects of the Christian faith are to be found in other religions. While today his work might be criticized as being facile and somewhat simplistic in suppressing the very real differences to be found in other religions, what is important is that he maintains an openness towards the possibility of salvation being found in these religions.

Again, with reference to the Inclusivist position, it is interesting to recall that Catholic theologians were anxious to point out that the "unconscious desire for Baptism", when found outside the Church, was sufficient for salvation. We find this, for example, in Thomas Aquinas.[16] Also, in the seventeenth century Rome condemned the Jansenists in France, who claimed that outside the Church there is no grace. In 1952, the Vatican excommunicated the American Jesuit, Father Feeney, who taught that all human beings who were outside the visible Catholic Church were condemned.

However, what really gave the impetus to this position of Inclusivism, particularly among Roman Catholic theologians, was the Second Vatican Council, in which, for the first time, there is clear and official recognition by the Church that salvation can be achieved outside the Church:

> Those who, through no fault of their own, do not know the Gospel of Christ or his Church but who nevertheless seek God with a sincere heart and, moved by grace, try in their actions to do his will as they know it through the dictates of their conscience — those too may achieve eternal salvation (*Lumen Gentium* 16).
>
> . . . in ways known to himself, God can lead those who, through no fault of their own, are ignorant of the Gospel to that faith without which it is impossible to please him (*Ad Gentes* 7).

(Sharing in the paschal mystery) holds true not for Christians only but also for all men of good will in whose hearts grace is active invisibly. For since Christ died for all, and since all men are in fact called to one and the same destiny, which is divine, we must hold that the Holy Spirit offers to all the possibility of being made partners, in a way known to God, in the paschal mystery (*Gaudium et Spes* 22).

The Catholic Church rejects nothing of what is true and holy in these religions. She has a high regard for the manner of life and conduct, the precepts and doctrines which, although differing in many ways from her own teaching, nevertheless often reflect a ray of that truth which enlightens all men (*Nostra Aetate* 2).

So the question is not, can individuals be saved outside the Church — that they can is no longer denied but rather explicitly affirmed by the highest authority in the Church; the question is: can they be saved *in* and *through* their own religions and not in spite of them? Various Catholic theologians hold that they can. Probably the most influential of them has been the late Karl Rahner, and his famous theory of "anonymous Christians".[17] Here we will not go into an analysis of Rahner's theory[18] but simply state that it must be presented with all the nuances which Rahner himself attached to it. Other Catholic theologians following this position to a greater or lesser degree are Thils,[19] Daniélou,[20] Küng (at least in his earlier writings),[21] Panikkar[22] and others.

The opponents of the Inclusivistic theory point out that it would seem to end up undermining the significance of the Incarnation. In so emphasizing the universality of salvation the uniqueness of Christ seems to have faded somewhat into the background. Likewise, it would seem to lessen the necessity of conversion. If salvation is to be found in and through other religions — albeit through the instrumentality of Christ — what is the point of preaching Christianity? What is so special about it? Over twenty years ago, when this theory was first presented to a group of missionaries in India, one missionary is reported to have stood up from the floor of the house and said: "Theologians, you are taking away from us what has all along been the main motive of our apostolic zeal! You tell us that non-Christians are being saved outside Christ's Church and that their religions are for them channels of grace. Why, then, disturb their good faith? And what have we come to do? To preach Christ or to make Hindus better Hindus and Muslims better Muslims? For me, I will go on converting, baptizing, and from today I will also pray for the conversion of theologians!"[23] There is no doubt that he put his point clearly.

Like Exclusivism, Inclusivism would also seem to function independently of any serious examination of the claims of other religions. Some would claim that it is an exploitation of non-Christian religions by Christianity. It could be argued that the issue has been prejudged and that "this line of approach represents a refusal to take seriously the other faiths on their own terms."[24]

Its proponents claim that it manages to maintain the tension between two aspects: the universality of God's salvific will and the centrality of Christ for salvation. It is because of this latter point that the approach is sometimes referred to as the Christocentric approach. Christ, the Word, is present throughout the world and active in the hearts of men and therefore they can be saved. Because humanity is, of its very nature, social and religions are the expression of the individuals' orientation towards the transcendent, it is logical to suppose that the ordinary means by which salvation is communicated to the individual is through the social aspect of the particular religion to which he or she belongs.

Pluralism

This brings us to the third approach, the Pluralist. This can be summed up in the phrase that all religions are equally valid paths to the one goal. In other words, Christianity is but one more way to God among the many that have appeared and are appearing in the world. The proponents of this approach argue that it is the only one that does justice to the claims of all religions. It resolves the tension between the universal salvific will of God and the claim to absoluteness of Christianity by stressing that what is essential is God. Thus it does not admit of ecclesiocentrism like the Exclusivists or Christocentrism like the Inclusivists but opts rather for Theocentrism. Pannikar prefers the word "parallelism" for this approach and presents it in the following words:

> If your religion appears far from being perfect and yet represents for you a symbol of the right path and a similar conviction seems to be the case for others, if you cannot dismiss the religious claim of the other nor assimilate it completely into your tradition, a plausible alternative is to assume that all are different creeds which, in spite of meanderings and crossings, actually run parallel to meet only in the ultimate, in the *eschaton*, at the very end of the human pilgrimage. Religions would then be parallel paths and our most urgent duty would be not to interfere with others, not to convert them or even to borrow from them, but to deepen our own respective traditions so that we meet at the end, and in the depths of our own tradition.[25]

The English theologian, John Hick, is probably the best known exponent of this position and has expounded it in numerous books and articles.[25] He claims that the Christian "monopoly of saving truth" is a price too high to pay and that it is a presumption which has "generated the paradox of a God of universal love who has ordained that only the Christian minority of the human race can be saved."[27] As regards the other religions he writes:

> Around the different ways of conceiving, experiencing and responding to the Real there have grown up the various religious traditions of the world with their myths and symbols, their philosophies and theologies, their liturgies and arts, their ethics and life-styles. Within all of them basically the same salvific process is taking place, namely, the transformation of human existence from self-centredness to Reality centredness. Each of the great traditions thus constitutes a valid context of salvation/liberation; each may be able to gain a larger understanding of the Real by attending to the reports and conceptualities of the others.[28]

Hick would claim that in order to understand the relationship between the different religions we must shift the

centre of our view of religions from Christ to God. He
would claim that our theological view in this matter is similar
to that of the Ptolomaic view of the universe before Coper-
nicus, seeing the earth as the centre of our system with all
the other planets seen in relation to it. "We have to realize",
he writes, "that the universe of faith centres upon *God* and
not upon Christianity or any other religion. He is the sun,
the original source of light and life, whom all the religions
reflect in their own different ways."[29]

The biblical basis, or rather argumentation, to which the
holders of this position usually refer are such texts as Genesis
8:20–9:17, Yahweh's covenant with Noah. With reference
to the covenant with Noah, Walbert Bühlmann has written:

> In the covenant with Noah we can see the legitimation, on
> the part of God, of all the extra-Israelite religions. For the
> biblical authors, the "pagan" peoples and the people of Israel
> share the same God as partners and both enjoy (although in
> a different way) his same bountiful salvific will. With the cove-
> nant of creation and that of Noah, God has shown that all
> peoples are his, and to all he shows the rainbow as a sign of
> hope.[30]

Donald G. Dawe writes in a similar vein:

> The Hebrew flood story, with its evident roots in the
> Gilgamesh Epic, becomes a myth of divine judgement and new
> creation in the Book of Genesis. Noah, the just one, is saved
> along with his family from the flood to be the basis for a new
> beginning in which God pledges his fidelity to all creation. After
> the flood, God establishes a covenant through Noah with
> "every living creature of all flesh" (Gen 9:15) in which he pro-
> mises never again to destroy the world in judgement. . . The
> crucial thing to remember is that the covenant of Noah is not
> conditional upon the response of men and women to it. It is
> clearly recognized that human beings are sinners and will
> remain such, a fact that Noah and his sons abundantly prove
> right after the flood. The covenant is made on the initiative
> of God and is sustained by God's faithfulness, despite human
> sin. This covenant reaches through Noah not only to "every
> living creature" but also to "all future generations".[31]

In the New Testament the Pluralists refer above all to the

general attitude of openness on the part of Jesus towards people of other faiths, for example, to the Samaritan woman and to the Roman officer, and to the fact that Jesus held up as an example of spirituality the behaviour of a Samaritan. They will also point out that Jesus himself did not preach his own centrality but rather the centrality of the kingdom of God, and this formed the essential kernel of his preaching.

Paul Knitter has expressed his preference for the Pluralist paradigm in his book *No Other Name?*[32] In it he writes: "The new model of relational truth provides the framework and incentive to strive toward. . . the direction of our new religious age: a unitive pluralism of religions. The understanding of truth as relational confirms. . . that, although there are real and important differences among the religions, differences that must be affirmed and confronted if dialogue is to bear fruit, these differences are, fundamentally, not contradictions but 'dialogical tensions and creative polarities' (Panikkar). The world religions, in all their amazing differences, are more complementary than contradictory."[33] According to him, "Christianity, along with all other religions, is evolving out of the *micro phase* of religious history in which the various traditions grew and consolidated in relative isolation from each other. The direction today is toward a *macro phase* of history in which each religion will be able to grow and understand itself only through interrelating with other religions."[34] In another place we find the following: "As the myth of the tower of Babel suggests, pluralism may be God's will. The *verum* (truth) may not be identical with the *unum* (one) (Pannikar). More concretely and uncomfortably, Buddhism or Hinduism may be as important for the history of salvation as is Christianity – or other revealers and saviours may be as important as Jesus of Nazareth. Yes, this is a crossroads."[35] He argues that the centre has moved from Christ, from the Church and even from God and that salvation is the true starting point, the true centre. "The evolution in Catholic theology of religions. . . must therefore move beyond theocentrism to *soteriocentrism*." [36]

Paul Tillich, speaking at Columbia University in 1961, said that Christianity must take seriously its universality and that means negating itself as a religion.

> The religious principle cannot come to an end. For the question of ultimate meaning of life cannot be silenced as long as men are men. Religion cannot come to an end and a particular religion will be lasting to the degree in which it negates itself as a religion. Thus Christianity will be a bearer of the new religious answer as long as it breaks through its own particularity.
> The way to achieve this is not to relinquish one's religious tradition for the sake of a universal concept which would be nothing but a concept. The way is to penetrate into the depths of one's own religion, in devotion, thought and action. In the depth of every living religion there is a point at which the religion itself loses its importance and that to which it points breaks through its particularity, elevating it to spiritual freedom and with it to a vision of the spiritual presence in other expressions of the ultimate meaning of man's existence.
> This is what Christianity must see in the present encounter of the world religions.[37]

There is something extraordinarily attractive in the Pluralist model. It seems to be in tune with our modern sensibilities in a way that the other two are not. It would seem to be more in harmony with true *Christian* charity and humility, more in line with the *Christian* understanding of God and of his plan for the salvation of all humanity, less prone to arrogance, triumphalism and that condescending attitude towards other faiths and cultures which has not infrequently characterized Christians in the past. At the same time, one cannot but ask whether, in so broadening our openness towards other religions, have we in the process emptied Christianity of its specifically *Christian* character? Has the Pluralist model not thrown out the baby with the bath-water? If all religions are equally true, can they not also be equally false? Is Christ any longer the centre of our faith? Does not the Pluralist paradigm force us to abandon our faith in the salvation of all mankind in and through Jesus Christ? Does it not force us to abandon our faith in Jesus, who is not only the Son of God but is the *only-begotten* Son of God, who is not only *a* Saviour but is *the* Saviour? Does not the Pluralist model introduce a relativism which in the long run would lead to the abandonment of all religion?

These and similar questions force us to re-examine our commitment as Christians, re-examine our faith and our response to it in the light of the challenge of other world religions. This situation can be very enriching for our own understanding of Christianity but what we cannot do is "assume or concede. . . that God has acted equally in and through every major world faith. For specifically Christian faith is committed to the belief that the Christ-event represents a decisive breakthrough in the history of religions."[38] One cannot hope to re-examine our faith in a fully complete manner in a work of this size or scope. It would mean examining the whole deposit of our faith as enshrined in the Bible, in Tradition and as explicitated by the Magisterium down through the centuries — something that is outside the range of this work as well as being outside the competence of its author. All I would hope to do is to examine briefly some few key themes in the light of their relationship to peoples of other religions. I do so from within the Christian faith, as a believer in Jesus Christ and as a missionary of Jesus Christ, one sent to witness to him. I write, not for the professional theologians but for my fellow missionaries, who are battling with the questions raised in their day-to-day existence, trying to be faithful to the Message they were sent to proclaim and at the same time trying to be totally respectful of the people to whom they proclaim it; trying, in other words, to be faithful to the commandment to love. I do not think that I have the answers to the questions posed but I feel that one can pose the questions without fear and hopefully, in clarifying the questions, one might draw a little nearer to the answers.

NOTES

1. Walter Kasper, "Are Non-Christian Religions Salvific?", in Mariasusai Dhavamony (ed.), *Evangelization, Dialogue and Development* (Gregoriana, Documenta Missionalia 5, Rome 1972) p. 157.

2. In an address at the opening of the Centre for Indian and Inter-Religious Studies in Rome on 15 September 1977, published in Thomas A. Aykara (ed.), *Meeting of Religions. New Orientations and Perspectives* (Dharmaram Publications, Bangalore 1978), p. 15.

3. Harold Coward, *Pluralism – Challenge to World Religions* (Orbis Books, Maryknoll, New York 1985), p. 13.

4. R. P. C. Hanson, *The Attractiveness of God. Essays in Christian Doctrine* (SPCK, London 1973), p. 9.

5. See: Gerald H. Anderson, "A Moratorium on Missionaries?", in Gerald H. Anderson & Thomas F. Stransky (eds.), *Mission Trends* 1 (Paulist Press, New York 1974), pp. 133–143.

6. See: Gustave Thils, *A "Non-Religious" Christianity* (Alba House, Staten Island, New York 1970). Here we find a discussion of the relationship between Christianity and religion and the views held on this topic by Karl Barth, Dietrich Bonhoeffer and Harvey Cox.

7. Homily on Joshua 3, 5.

8. Epistle 73, 21.

9. Hendrik Kraemer, *The Christian Message in a Non-Christian World* (Edinburgh House Press, London 1938), pp. 113–114.

10. A particularly fine study of the Tradition of the Fathers in this regard is that of Chrys Saldhana, *A Patristic View on Non-Christian Religions* (Libreria Ateneo Salesiano, Rome 1984). See also: James Dupuis, "The Cosmic Christ in the Early Fathers", in *Indian Journal of Theology* 1966, pp. 106–120.

11. Raymond Panikkar, *The Intrareligious Dialogue* (Paulist Press, New York 1978), p. xv.

12. See: Karl Barth, Church Dogmatics, vol. 1/II: "The Doctrine of the Word of God", trans. G. T. Thomson & H. Knight (Charles Scribner's, New York 1956), pp. 299ff. Barth held that "the revelation of God is the abolition of religion". Revelation for him is the assumption (*Aufhebung*) of religion. For him true revelation and religion are opposed, for religion is man's attempt to find God, to find salvation, while revelation is God's self-disclosure, God's offer of salvation, and only he can save.

13. Alan Race, *Christians and Religious Pluralism – Patterns in the Christian Theology of Religions* (Orbis Books, Maryknoll, New York 1982), p. 38.

14. First Apology XLVI.

15. *Stromata* VI, 2.

16. S. Th. III, q. 68, a. 2; q. 66, a. 11f.

17. On this subject, see: Karl Rahner, "Anonymous Christians", *Theological Investigations VI* (Darton, Longman and Todd, London 1969), pp. 390–398; "Atheism and Implicit Christianity", *Theological Investigations IX* (1972), pp. 145–164; "Anonymous Christianity and Missionary Task

of the Church"; *Theological Investigations XII* (1974), pp. 161–178; "Jesus Christ in the Non-Christian Religions", *Theological Investigations XVII* (1981). See also his article on "Mission", in *Sacramentum Mundi* III (Seabury Press, New York, 1969), pp. 547–551.

18. This has been very well done by Klaus Riesenhuber, "Der anonyme Christ nach K. Rahner", in *Zeitschr. f. Kath. Theol.* 86 (1964), pp. 276–303.

19. See his *Propos et Problèmes de la Théologie des Religions Non-Chrétiennes*, Tournai 1966.

20. A short exposition of his ideas can be found in his article "Christianity and Non-Christian Religions", in T. P. Burke (ed.), *The Word in History*, (New York 1966), pp. 86ff. Also in Maurice Eminyan, *The Theology of Salvation* (St. Paul Editions, Boston 1960), pp. 140–149.

21. E.g., *On Being a Christian* (Collins, London 1977), pp. 89–96; also his "The World Religions in God's Plan of Salvation", in *Indian Ecclesiastical Review* 4 (1965).

22. E.g., *The Unknown Christ of Hinduism* (Darton, Longman and Todd, London, and Orbis Books, Maryknoll, N.Y., 1981, rev. ed.) and "The Meaning of Christ's Name in the Universal Economy of Salvation", in Mariasusai Dhavamony (ed.), *Evangelization, Dialogue and Development*, pp. 195–218.

23. Cf. P. Fallon, "The Church and the World Religions", in *The Clergy Monthly*, India, Vol, XXIX, 6, June 1965, p. 231.

24. Alan Race, *Christians and Religious Pluralism: Patterns in the Christian Theology of Religions*, p. 56.

25. Raymond Panikkar, *The Intrareligious Dialogue*, p. xviii.

26. For example, John Hick, "The Non-Absoluteness of Christianity", in John Hick and Paul F. Knitter, *The Myth of Christian Uniqueness* (Orbis Books, Maryknoll, N.Y., 1987 and SCM, London 1988), pp. 16–36. *Problems of Religious Pluralism* (Macmillan, New York, 1985) (a collection of previously published articles). See particularly the article entitled "In Defence of Religious Pluralism", pp. 96–109; "Jesus and the World Religions", in John Hick (ed.) *The Myth of God Incarnate* (SCM, London 1977), pp. 167–185. "Whatever Path Men Choose is Mine", in John Hick and Brian Hebblethwaite (eds.), *Christianity and Other Religions* (Fortress, Philadelphia 1980), pp. 171–190.

27. "In Defence of Religious Pluralism", p. 99.

28. *Ibid.,* p. 102

29. In "Whatever Path Men Choose is Mine", *Christianity and Other Religions*, p. 182. In a recent newspaper article he wrote: "(The) pluralist vision must, like the acceptance of evolution a hundred years ago, involve a development of Christian belief; but the Christian tradition has always in practice been a tradition of growth in response to the changing pressures of history. In the one world of modern communications, and of a fateful political and economic interdependence, new Christian possibilities must be allowed to come to the fore." (*The Independent*, London, 27 May 1989.)

30. Walbert Bühlmann, *The Chosen Peoples* (St Paul Publications, Slough 1982 and *God's Chosen Peoples*, Orbis Books, Maryknoll, N.Y. 1982), pp. 26–27.

31. "Christian Faith in a Religiously Plural World", in Donald G. Dawe

and John B. Carmen (eds.), *Christian Faith in a Religiously Plural World*, (Orbis Books, Maryknoll, N.Y. 1978), pp. 19–20.

32. Paul Knitter, *No Other Name? A Critical Survey of Christian Attitudes Toward the World Religions* (Orbis Books, Maryknoll, N.Y. 1985). See also his article "Catholic Theology of Religions at a Crossroads", in *Concilium*, February 1986, pp. 99–107, and "Toward a Liberation Theology of Religions", in *The Myth of Christian Uniqueness*, pp. 178–200.

33. *No Other Name?*, p. 220.

34. *Ibid.*, p. 225.

35. "Catholic Theology of Religions at a Crossroads", *Concilium*, p. 103.

36. *Ibid.*, p. 105.

37. Paul Tillich, *Christianity and the Encounter of the World Religions* (Columbia University Press, New York and London 1963), pp. 96–97.

38. Brian Hebblethwaite, *The Incarnation* (Cambridge University Press, Cambridge 1987) p. 111.

2

Salvation

It can be argued that, of all religious terms, "salvation" is the most comprehensive and that almost all religions can be seen as expressions of the universal seeking after salvation in some form or other. However, what we are saved from, and what salvation consists of, are understood differently in the various religions. For example, most Buddhists would see salvation as consisting in the release from suffering and desire, which is to be attained through higher knowledge.[1] For the majority of Hindus salvation lies in the liberation from the relentless cycle of rebirth and in the complete submergence of the individual self in the Eternal Self.[2] Indeed, "salvation" is one of those words which in recent years have become highly controversial both within and outside Christian circles. For many in our Western World, especially among the young, it has become meaningless, irrelevant, vacuous. Even for those who would admit being Christians "salvation", in the traditional sense of the term, is simply no longer of vital concern. The saving of one's soul, the "deliverance from sin" or the "admission into eternal bliss" are no longer seen by many as vital issues. Work, food, shelter, leisure, the weekly wage packet, the threat of nuclear destruction, the preservation of our environment – such are the issues that interest the average Western man or woman. For them, the traditional presentation of salvation in Christian theology is largely unintelligible.

Yet, it is equally clear that modern man is still striving to solve the enigma of human existence, still searching for answers to the basic questions of life, which include: where have I come from? Why am I on earth? Where am I going to? How am I to get there? Some have tried to give purely human answers to these questions. Humanity, they feel, has come of age, is now an adult, and no longer needs God to answer the questions of life. Man, they would claim, finds his own salvation, within himself, within herself, and the explanations of man's deepest longings are to be sought in the realms of psychology and sociology. Nevertheless, as we approach the end of the second millennium of our Christian era, it must be admitted that an ever-increasing number is discovering once again that salvation cannot be merely human. Despite the claims of some psychoanalysts and political movements, salvation cannot be achieved by humanity's own efforts; in order to be truly salvation, it must transcend man. So there is the turning to religion for the answers, and not only in the so-called Third and Fourth Worlds but also in the First and Second Worlds. People are seeking an explanation for the ever-present conviction that each individual's life is ultimately good and meaningful. Humanity recoils at the idea that a human life is a "useless passion" and it will not accept that "it is absurd that we are born and it is absurd that we die."[3] The increase in the number of students taking religious studies in our European colleges and universities (and who are not preparing for ministry in the different denominations) is indicative. There is a marked proliferation of books and articles on such topics as the occult, astrology, methods of meditation, as well as the constant rise of new religions and the rediscovery of old ones – all this is an indication of the growing interest in religion and the search for salvation. So, within Christianity at least, theologians and pastors have sought for other equivalent terms with which to express their understanding of the reality behind the term "salvation" in the hope of thereby making it more comprehensible to the people of today.[4] Some terms put forward are the traditional ones like "redemption", "eternal life", "the kingdom of God"; others, more modern sounding but also with a good foundation in Scripture, are terms such as "liberation", "wholeness", "fullness", "shalom". The very multiplicity of such equivalents helps to underline the complexity of the concept.

God alone saves

In its ordinary usage in the English language, the word "salvation" normally refers to the idea of "being saved, rescued from some actual or impending danger". Thus we speak of "being saved" from a fire, from a car accident, from drowning, etc. People say, "His good relationship with his boss was his salvation", or, "The policeman owes his salvation to his bullet-proof vest." What is emphasized is the aspect of being saved *from* something. This somewhat negative connotation is carried over into the religious field, and when in the Christian context people talk about salvation what is uppermost in their minds is, more often than not, the ideal of being saved from sin, from death, from hell. It cannot be denied that this aspect of salvation is of vital importance. It helps to underline the fact that salvation has to do with the concrete reality of our historical existence. It brings home to us in a powerful way that salvation is indeed something that concerns this world here and now, something that has to do with our real life, our situation here and now in this world. That is why we have traditionally looked upon salvation as redemption – redemption from the incompleteness or lack of wholeness which is experienced in the very depths of human existence and in every aspect of it.

However, there is another aspect of salvation that must be taken into account. Recently, Pope John Paul II put it in these words:

> Because salvation is a total and integral reality, it concerns man and all men, and touches as well historical and social reality, culture and community structures in which they live. However, salvation cannot be confined to the picture of merely the earthly necessities of man or of society, neither can it be reached by playing with historical dialectics. Man is not his own saviour in a definitive manner; salvation transcends that which is human and earthly – it is a gift from above. There is no self-redemption; God alone saves man in Christ.[5]

The notion of salvation as "deliverance" must be

balanced by the notion of salvation as a blessing bestowed on mankind by a gracious and loving God. It is always the freely given grace of God. The Greek word for salvation, "*soteria*",[6] helps to bring this idea out as do also some other European languages. For example, the German word, "*heil*", or the French "*salut*" and the Spanish "*salud*", all bring out clearly the intimate connection between salvation and "health" or "well-being" thereby emphasizing the positive side of salvation. Salvation has to do with the perfection of one's being, with healing, wholeness, "admission into eternal bliss", to use the traditional phrase. Salvation seen as a blessing underlines the fact that it is not only a temporal reality but also an eternal one, something planned and willed by God from all eternity. It is not just a case of salvation *from* something but also salvation *for* something. To sum up, we might say that salvation is God's blessing bestowed on humanity seen from its sinful, fallen situation.

Another point worthy of mention is that in our traditional use of the term "salvation" it tended to be presented and understood in a predominantly individualistic way. Each one was called to save his or her soul. "Save your soul" was the slogan and very little attention was given to man's social nature or the structures in which he lived. When this individualism is joined to the other-worldly orientation implied in the word "soul" (to the detriment of man's corporeal, material nature) Christianity lets itself be wide open to the "opium-of-the-people" accusation. Religion could therefore be seen as an escape from commitment to this world, a means of strengthening the mentality of "accepting one's lot" — even when that lot is manifestly grossly unjust. Salvation has however to do with the whole human being seen in his or her individuality and sociability.

Salvation as deliverance and fulfilment

In order to appreciate fully the Christian concept of salvation it is important to consider first of all its understanding of evil. When we observe the world and man's situation within it, we are immediately conscious that there is something radically wrong. We see that man is a being divided within himself, at odds with himself, with the created world about him, with his fellow brothers or sisters and with God. Humanity finds its deepest longings and desires frustrated. Man and woman long for life and happiness but all around they encounter death and sorrow. They want peace and fraternity but find, in its stead, war, aggression, brother against brother, sister against sister, family against family, nation against nation. They long for union with the source of their being but find themselves unable to achieve it. The human existential situation is thus seen as fundamentally a rupture of relationships. Firstly, a rupture in our relationship with creation – and particularly that part of creation closest to us, our own bodies, manifesting itself in sickness, old age, death. Secondly, there is the rupture in our relationship with others, so often marked by broken friendships, betrayals, divorce, enmity, jealousy, war. Finally, there is the rupture in our relationship with God, experienced in our consciousness of being sinners, guilty, alienated, egoistic and alone. It is in the light of this background and understanding of evil that the Christian concept of salvation as enshrined in the Bible must be understood. As Yves Congar has pointed out: "The Bible and the tradition within which the Church has lived it present the fact of salvation both as deliverance or rescue and as fulfilment."[7]

Salvation in the Old Testament

When we look at the Old Testament the concept of salvation that emerged among the people of Israel was a concept formed over many years and was based on their experience of Yahweh and his dealings with them. In the first place, they experienced being saved by him as a people, as a community. And secondly, they experienced him active in their individual lives. It was Yahweh who had delivered them from slavery in Egypt, who had fought on their behalf against their foes and won for them possession of the Promised Land. He it was who had led them through the desert. "And the Lord went before them by day in a pillar of cloud to lead them along the way, and by night in a pillar of fire to give them light" (Ex 13:21). It was he who had led them back to their homeland after the exile and despite their infidelities had not abandoned them. Yahweh was their "rock" and their "salvation", their security, their God who had made a covenant with them, according to which he would commit himself to them on condition that they accepted him as their God, accepted him as their Leader. He was their King, their Shepherd, in whom they could place absolute trust and confidence. They themselves were a stiff-necked and disobedient people, totally incapable of winning their liberation from slavery, of entering the Promised Land. They were sinners; so salvation was something that they had never earned. It was totally the result of the goodness of God, his love for them, and nothing else. Moreover, he cared for them, not only as a community, as his people, but also as individuals. The sick man, the childless wife, the orphan and the stranger, all could have recourse to him in their personal needs. He would be their Advocate in the courts, their Physician in their illnesses, their Protector in times of danger. To him the just, the meek, the poor, the little ones, the persecuted and the downcast could turn with complete confidence. Over and over again, their cry is, "Save us, Yahweh!"

Salvation in the New Testament

In the New Testament all these ideas are enriched and fulfilled in Christ. He is *the* Saviour, *Soter*, the one in whom God's love for man manifests itself in all its fullness. Edward Schillebeeckx has written beautifully about Christ as the Saviour.[8] He writes:

> In their experience of the meaning of life and its fulfilment, the disciples experience salvation from God in their trusting encounter with Jesus. This determination of life as an unmerited gift, as grace, is experienced as the initiative of God

which surpasses all expectations. Here Old and New Testaments are agreed: Yahweh is a God of man, he is the "He is" (Ex 3:14), i.e., "I am concerned for you" (Ex 3:16). God's name is "solidarity with my people". God's own honour lies in the happiness and salvation of mankind. God's predestination and man's experience of meaning are two aspects of one and the same reality of salvation. Salvation is concerned with human wholeness and happiness and this is in an intrinsic mutual relationship involving the solidarity of man with a living God who is concerned with mankind.[9]

And in another place we find:

The meaning or the destiny of man, prepared for and intended from of old by God, has been disclosed and thus made known in an experience of believers in the person, career and destiny of Jesus of Nazareth: in his message and his life, his life-style and the particular circumstances in which he was executed. Such a life and death have value *in and of themselves*. But for that very reason they also have a primary significance for God, who here shows his own solidarity with his people, their own calling and their own honour and therefore identifies himself not only with the ideals and visions of Jesus but with the person of Jesus of Nazareth himself. Thus the destiny of Jesus is fulfilled even beyond death in his resurrection from the dead, the Amen of God to the person of Jesus which is at the same time the divine affirmation of his true being: "solidarity with the people", "God is love" (1 Jn 4:8; 4:16).[10]

He points out that in the man Jesus, God's history becomes our history. He writes:

By following Jesus, taking our bearings from him and allowing ourselves to be inspired by him, by sharing in his *Abba* experience and his selfless support for "the least of my brethren" (Mt 25:40) and thus entrusting our own destiny to God, we allow the history of Jesus, the living one, to continue in history as a piece of living Christology, the work of the Spirit among us, the Spirit of God and the Spirit of Christ. So the Christian works in free responsibility for the completion of God's plan to give ultimate meaning to human life. This is the means of achieving the correlation between God's will for universal salvation in Jesus and for human happiness or success for each and every individual.[11]

For the Christian, soteriology and Christology cannot be separated; one cannot separate the work of Christ from the person of Christ. Christ is at the heart of the salvation of all mankind, precisely because, as Yves Congar has pointed out, he "*is* the substantial union of man and God. There cannot exist a religious relation more perfect than that which he realized in himself and which he realizes in us: the absolute filial relation."[12] Jesus signifies Saviour and his actions are saving actions. In his teaching he continually emphasized the infinite value of each individual and the fact that his mission was "to seek and to save the lost" (Lk 19:10). "I did not come to judge the world but to save the world" (Jn 12:47). He speaks that men might be saved (cf. Jn 5:34). He reminds us that not even one sparrow "is forgotten before God" and that even the hairs of our head "are all numbered" (Lk 12:6-7). By his miracles of healing he underlines that salvation, *soteria*, includes physical as well as spiritual healing, that it has to do with wholeness. He fully assumes the biblical anthropological tradition of the total unity of man, body-soul. By his life, death and resurrection Jesus heals the broken relationships of mankind, bringing about reconciliation between God and man, between man and man, and between man and creation. In Jesus himself salvation has come. Jesus Christ, his life, death and resurrection is what gives definitive meaning to man's existence here on earth.[13] What the risen Jesus now is — that is what each one is called to be. Jesus is the destiny of each and every human being. In him is fulfilled all of mankind's longing. In Jesus, God offers to humanity the gift of wholeness, integrity, the gift of freedom, the freedom to be fully and truly man, the freedom to be what God has called us to be.

When the Second Person of the Blessed Trinity became man God took to himself man's finitude, man's sin and fallen situation. He identified himself with man's suffering and in doing so liberated man from his bondage. For that reason Jesus is the sacrament of man's salvation, that is, Jesus is the *sign* of man's salvation and the *instrument* whereby it is effected. "Salvation", therefore, signifies not just a saving from condemnation because of our sinfulness, because of our rebellion against God, but it is also the attainment of our destiny, the attainment of that for which we were created. The Gospel is therefore "the message of this salvation" (Acts 13:26) and the "way of salvation" (Acts 16:17).

It is therefore constitutive of the Christian faith that salvation is brought about in and through Jesus Christ, that in him God realized his salvific plan and that this plan affects all creation and all men of all ages.

> The mystery of Christ guarantees not only the salvation of man but also the salvation of the world and of history. Through man, the world is also called to share in the glory of Christ (Rom 8:19-23). The saving power of Christ extends to all creation and will reach its plenitude when all is recapitulated in him (1 Cor 8:6; 15:25-28, Eph 1:9-10, Col 1:15-18). History will achieve its final plenitude in the glorified Christ.[14]

Irenaeus, writing towards the end of the second century, had expressed the same idea:

> Now it has been clearly demonstrated that the Word which exists from the beginning with God, by whom all things were made, who was also present with the race of men at all times, this Word has in these last times, according to the time appointed by the Father, been united to his own workmanship and has been made passible man. Therefore we can set aside the objection of them that say, 'If he was born at that time it follows that Christ did not exist before then.' For we have shown that the Son of God did not then begin to exist, since he existed with the Father always; but when he was incarnate and made man, he recapitulated (*or*: summed up) in himself the long line of the human race, procuring for us salvation thus summarily, so that what we had lost in Adam, that is, the being in the image and likeness of God, that we should regain in Christ Jesus.[15]

And again:

> . . . This is why the Lord declares himself to be the Son of Man, because he recapitulates (sums up) in himself the original man who was the source from which sprang the race fashioned

after woman; that as through the conquest of man our race went down to death, so through the victory of man we might ascend to life.[16]

Christ is, therefore, the personal Totality of God's plan of salvation. The working out of this plan in space and time forms the history of salvation which can be seen as consisting of three stages or, if one prefers, as being realized on three levels: on the level of creation, on the level of his special revelation to Israel and finally and conclusively in Jesus Christ. Vatican II expressed this faith in the following words:

> God, who through the Word creates all things (cf. Jn 1:3) and keeps them in existence, gives men an enduring witness to himself in created realities (cf. Rom 1:19-20). Planning to make known the way of heavenly salvation, he went further and from the start manifested himself to our first parents. Then after their fall his promise of redemption aroused in them the hope of being saved (cf. Gen 3:15) and from that time on ceaselessly kept the human race in his care, in order to give eternal life to those who perseveringly do good in search of salvation (cf. Rom 2:6-7). Then, at the time he had appointed, he called Abraham in order to make of him a great nation (cf. Gen 12:2). Through the patriarchs, and after them through Moses and the prophets, he taught this nation to acknowledge himself as the one living and true God, provident Father and just judge, and to wait for the Saviour promised by him. In this manner he prepared the way for the Gospel down through the centuries (Dogmatic Constitution on Divine Revelation, *Dei Verbum* 3).

And this salvific will of God is universal. The God who is goodness itself, who is the creator of all mankind, desires the salvation of all. The New Testament states it in quite unambiguous terms: God "desires all men to be saved and to come to the knowledge of the truth. For there is one God, and there is one mediator between God and men, the man Christ Jesus" (1 Tim 2:4-5). "And there is salvation in no one else, for there is no other name under heaven given among men by which we must be saved" (Acts 4:12). "He did not say this of his own accord, but being high priest that year he prophesied that Jesus should die for the nation, and not for the nation only, but to gather into one the children of God who are scattered abroad'' (Jn 11:51-52). "I tell you, many will come from east and west and sit at table with Abraham, Isaac and Jacob in the kingdom of heaven" (Mt 8:11). In this connection we also recall the final chapter of Jonah with its message of God's universal mercy on all his creatures represented by the inhabitants of Nineveh. Likewise in Isaiah, "And there is no other god besides me, a righteous God and a Saviour; there is none besides me. Turn to me and be saved, all the ends of the earth" (45:21-22).

Is salvation possible only within the Church?

This brings us directly to our specific theme: since Christ is *the* Saviour and since "there is salvation in no one else, for there is no other name under heaven given among men by which we must be saved" (Acts 4:12), how then can the followers of other religions who do not accept or even specifically reject Christ and the claims of Christianity be saved? How can the other religions be vehicles of salvation for their adherents? Again, it must be recalled that I am viewing the question from within the Christian standpoint only, from within the framework of the life situation of a believer in Jesus Christ and in his Gospel. In this context, the question is, does Christianity *exclude* the other religions as vehicles of salvation? Of course, we know and accept that God can save people of other faiths, but is this salvation effected *in spite of* their religion or *in* and *through* their religion? In other words, from the standpoint of Christianity (and that means keeping in mind the two poles of the argument: the unique role of Christ as the universal Saviour and the universal salvific will of God) can other religions be, in themselves, salvific for their adherents?

While it would seem that it is not possible to give a full and completely satisfactory answer to this question, there are certain points that need to be kept in mind in order to have a balanced view of the problem. The first point is that salvation must not be seen in terms of the Incarnation exclusively. We must always maintain the intimate link between the redemption effected by Christ and God's plan of salvation initiated in creation. "All things are created by him and for him and they tend towards him in order to realize their end through him, which is to manifest God."[17] Unfortunately there has been a tendency to separate creation and Incarnation. This is particularly so when salvation is seen exclusively as a "rescue" exercise and the "blessing" aspect is forgotten. When this latter aspect is taken into account then salvation is seen as something that is present in God's plan right from the very beginning. When we dissociate the two we end up with all sorts of complicated problems, not least of which is the absolutization of Christianity to such an extent that God is "unable" to work in any other way.

Creation and Incarnation have behind them the identical same motive force: God's grace. Both have the same appointed goal: participation in the supernatural life of God himself. The salvation brought about by Jesus Christ is the completion and perfection of the process initiated in creation. Christ the Redeemer is the same Christ in whom "all things were created, in heaven and on earth, visible and invisible, whether thrones or dominions or principalities or authorities — all things were created through him and for him. He is before all things and in him all things hold together" (Col 1:16-17). God's universal salvific will is present and active from all eternity. It was because God wanted to confer on humanity a blessing that he called it into existence. This universal salvific will acts, as it were, like a magnet within the heart of creation, drawing all things to their ultimate goal. For this reason creation is, to use the Pauline image, groaning with the pangs of childbirth. Creation theology underlines the fundamental equality of all human beings and this is necessary in order to act as a balance to the idea of favour and choice implied in the covenant concept of salvation. The salvific process begun at creation was not nullified by the Incarnation. On the contrary, Christ assumed it and brought it to perfection. He did not come to destroy but to fulfil (cf. Mt 5:17). The movement from *chaos* to *kosmos* to *theosis* is one continuous whole. This enables us to integrate all human striving towards God into the one movement without in any way denying the special place, the central place, that Christ occupies in it. The Incarnate Christ is the one through whom all things came to be, "and without him was not anything made that was made" (Jn 1:3).

God's plan of salvation is rooted in eternity but will come to its fullness only at the end of time and not before that. We look forward to a "salvation ready to be revealed in the last time" (1 Pet 1:5). There is a tension between the two aspects, between the eternal and the temporal, and it is vitally important that we maintain that tension. Over-emphasis of one aspect to the neglect of the other leads to distortion. If we so emphasize the eternal aspect at the expense of the temporal and historical there results a relativization of the role of Christ in salvation that is unacceptable.[18] Likewise, if we over-emphasize the historical and temporal aspect of God's plan of salvation there results an unacceptable absolutization of these aspects which expresses itself in an exclusivism and intolerance that is most unchristian. Maintaining the tension is an integral part of Christianity, and indeed of every aspect of it — between nature and grace, between the divine and the human, between the "already" and the "not yet". Awareness of the tension between the eternal and the temporal aspects of salvation helps us to accept and rejoice in the existence of salvation outside the visible boundaries of Christianity without in any way weakening one's commitment to Christianity or to its mission. Failure to maintain the tension has in the past, due to a one-sided emphasis on the historical, incarnational aspects of salvation, led to attitudes and deeds of intolerance, condemnation and superiority which are the very antithesis of the spirit of Jesus. Today, perhaps, there exists the danger of the other end of the pendulum swing: over-emphasis on the eternal aspect of salvation. Such an over-emphasis can easily lead to relativism, diminishment of apostolic zeal, failure to appreciate the extraordinary goodness of the Good News of Jesus Christ and even to the total abandonment of the fundamental mission of Christianity.

Another consideration which helps us to see and accept the presence of salvation in the world about us, without in any way abandoning or diluting our faith in the uniqueness and universality of Christ or the role and mission of the Church, is to rediscover the place of the Trinity in the saving process. It is of the very essence of our faith that salvation is brought about by God in Jesus Christ, that this saving ministry is continued by the Holy Spirit in and through the Church. Immediately someone will ask: what about that part of humanity — by far the largest part — which does not belong to the Church or which even explicitly rejects the Church? I will discuss this problem more at length when we come to speak of revelation and faith. At this juncture, suffice it to say that when we speak of the Holy Spirit continuing Christ's saving ministry through the Church we do not necessarily mean that he works *exclusively* through the Church. He is not tied. What the Spirit does is insert us into the reality of God — the God who is love — and it is this which enables us to go out of ourselves to others, to break down barriers, barriers of race, creed and cultures, to abandon the security of law in order to live in the freedom of love. This activity of the Spirit is found outside the frontiers of the Church.

The world exists because God, in his infinite wisdom and goodness, wished to share his own life and happiness with other personal beings. God the Father is the creator and the world is the result of his creative will. However, the full meaning of this world would be unknown to us had not God himself revealed it to us and this he did when he spoke his Word — the Word in which all his other "words" (creation) were already present. And this Word was made flesh, became man, Jesus, the son of Mary. In this man, Jesus, God himself was present, revealing himself and his plan, the meaning and why of creation. And Jesus was not merely the revealer of his plan, the revealer of God's blessing on his creation: Jesus was also the instrument by means of which this blessing was to be effected. All of this is, therefore, due to God's Spirit, the Holy Spirit, the bond, as it were, between the Father and the Son. And this Spirit of the Father and of the Son is there present at every moment of the plan.[19] To speak in human terms, he is at the heart of the plan. The work of salvation, that is, the work of creation plus redemption, is the work of the one eternal, omnipotent, omnipresent God who is Trinity; and as Trinity we tend to "associate" the Father with the origin of the plan of salvation, the Son with the execution of the plan and the Holy Spirit with the dynamism and continuation of it, while realizing that the one plan in its entirety is the work of the one God. Seeing the work of salvation in this way enables us to hold in tension the different elements of the plan without separating them from the overall unity. It also enables us to see the plan within the context of love, for the understanding of God as Trinity is precisely our way of expressing our understanding of God as love, love that is self-communicating, self-giving.

Interestingly enough, the problem of the relationship of Christianity to other religions arises precisely because of the specific understanding of God that is revealed in Christianity. If God had not revealed himself in Jesus Christ as love, then interpersonal relationships would not occupy the central position that they do in the Christian dispensation. Because we are created in the image of God, the God who is Trinity, the God that is in himself, relational, means that we can only find ourselves, can only fully *be* ourselves, in and through relationships.

These points, of course, do not solve the problem of what is the relationship between salvation and the other religions but I think that they do help us to have a more nuanced approach: more aware of the factors involved and less likely to take up positions which are ultimately either untrue to our faith, untrue to the command to love or untrue to the mission which we have received. If we keep in mind that God is the creator of the whole universe, that he created it so that *all* mankind might share with him his own happiness and life, and that this will of his is operative from the very first moment in which he chose to implement his plan, then it becomes much easier to accept the operation of this plan right from the very beginning and throughout the whole of creation, even though the central element of it — the life, death and resurrection of Christ — is historically and geographically confined. The plan of salvation has its dynamism, its power, in the presence of the Spirit. By keeping in mind the Trinitarian dimension of this plan, we make it easier to maintain in balance the creational aspect associated with the Father, the historical aspect associated with the Son and the continuing aspect associated with the Spirit.

NOTES

1. For a very short overview of salvation as it is found in Buddhism and other non-Christian religions, see Mariasusai Dhavamony, "Today's Challenge: Salvation Offered by Non-Christian Religions", in *La Salvezza Oggi* (Acts of the Fifth International Congress of Missiology held in Rome at the Pontifical Urban University, 5–8 October 1988 and published by the Urban University Press 1988), pp. 81–100.

2. Cf. Daniel Acharuparambil, "Hindu Salvation: A Human Conquest or a Divine Gift?" in *La Salvezza Oggi*, pp. 227–240.

3. J.-P. Sartre, *Being and Nothingness* (English translation, London 1957), p. 615.

4. See the fine article on "Salvation" in *Sacramentum Mundi*, Vol. V, (Herder & Herder, New York and Burns & Oates, London 1970).

5. Address to the participants of the above mentioned Congress. Printed in *Omnis Terra*, No. 193 (December 1988), p. 540.

6. For an examination of the words *soteria* (salvation) and *sozein* (to save) in the New Testament, see: W. Barclay, *A New Testament Workbook* (Harper, USA 1957 and London 1959), pp. 114–121.

7. Yves Congar, *The Wide World, My Parish* (English translation: Helicon Press, Baltimore 1961), p. 38.

8. Particularly in his book, *Christ. The Christian Experience in the Modern World* (English translation, SCM Press, London 1980).

9. *Ibid.*, p. 639.

10. *Ibid.*

11. *Ibid.*, pp. 641–642.

12. Yves Congar, "Non-Christian Religions and Christianity", in Mariasusai Dhavamony (ed.), *Evangelization, Dialogue and Development* (Documenta Missionalia 5, Gregorian University Press, Rome 1972), p. 135.

13. Cf. Karl Rahner, "Jesus Christ — the Meaning of Life", *Theological Investigations* Vol XXI (Darton, Longman and Todd, London 1988), pp. 208–219.

14. Juan Alfaro, *Christian Hope and the Liberation of Man*, (E. J. Dwyer, Rome and Sydney 1978), p. 36.

15. *Adv. haer.* III, xviii.

16. *Adv. haer.* V, xxi, 1.

17. Lucen Cerfaux, *Christ in the Theology of St Paul* (Herder and Herder, New York 1959), p. 430.

18. It could be argued that this can be found in some proponents of the Pluralist model of the relationship between the religions; for example, John Hick, who would deny the literal Incarnation of God in Jesus Christ. Cf. his book *God Has Many Names* (Westminster Press, Philadelphia 1980). Hick would stress that *for us* the best way to experience God is Jesus, but this is not necessarily so for all. "We can revere Christ as the one through whom we have found salvation, without having to deny other points of reported saving contact between God and man. We can commend the way of Christian faith without having to discommend other ways of faith. We can say that there is salvation in Christ without having to say that there is no salvation other than in Christ" (p. 75). See also: Alan Race, *Christians and Religious Pluralism – Patterns in the Christian Theology of Religions* (Orbis Books, Maryknoll, N.Y. 1982).

19. Cf. James Dupuis, "The Cosmic Influence of the Holy Spirit and the Gospel Message", in G. Gispert-Sauch (ed.), *God's Word Among Men*, (Delhi 1973), pp. 129–133. Also by James Dupuis, "The Cosmic Economy of the Spirit and the Sacred Scriptures of Religious Traditions", in D. S. Amalorpavadas (ed.), *Research Seminar on Non-Biblical Scriptures* (Bangalore 1974), pp. 117–135. Cf. also: Jacob Kavumkal, "Cosmic Economy of the Spirit and the Non-Christian Religions", in *Indian Missiological Review*, January 1981, pp. 19–28.

3

Revelation

Having looked briefly at the concept of salvation, it is logical that we should now pass on to consider the concept of revelation, for there is a close link between the two. Indeed, salvation can be seen as man's encounter with revelation, while revelation is manifested to the world primarily in categories of salvation. "Most intimately bound up with this self-revelation of God is the revelation of his *will* to men. . . This will at the same time signifies salvation *for* men. From the Protoevangelion to the fulfilment in Christ, the history of revelation is a salvation history."[1] Here it is not our purpose to write a treatise on revelation as it is understood within Christianity but merely to show how the concept can be seen in relation to peoples of other faiths and our mission to proclaim Christ to the whole world.

Despite Nietzsche's proclamation that "God is dead", humanity still continues to have a spiritual life, a life that surpasses the merely physical world in which we live. Men and women still seek answers to the questions of love and hate, birth and death, fear and joy. No doubt, there is a sense in which Nietzsche was perfectly right, in that a certain image of God, a certain way of conceiving God in accordance with a particular philosophical framework, is dead, and so it is necessary to renew our image of God and our way of speaking about him. As is well known, some people today, following in the footsteps of Fuerbach and Freud, would try to rid themselves of the God question altogether, saying that God is merely a creation of man's psyche, a projection which has its origin in man's fears and desires. Others, while willing to admit the possibility of God's existence would claim that it is impossible for man to form any idea of what is meant by the term "God", for

God is, by definition, the "totally Other", the completely hidden One.

What is revelation?

It is for this reason that the question of revelation has, in modern times, entered the centre of the theological arena. One author has claimed that "most discussions of revelation have created complex conceptual and epistemological tangles that are difficult to understand and nearly impossible to unravel."[2] Formerly, theologians tended to ask about the *content* of revelation, *what* is it that revelation makes known to us; today the question is, what is revelation *itself*? Revelation has been defined, or better, described in a number of ways.[3] And while being aware of the limitations of human language, here we will use the word "revelation" in its generally accepted connotation within Christian understanding. Christianity is based on the conviction that a *historical* revelation took place. Some religions are based on man's reflection on his existential situation and, from that, developing a set of beliefs upon which to orientate and give meaning to his life. Others believe that God has indeed revealed something to man but that this revelation was, as it were, dispersed, ahistorical. For Christianity, however, revelation took place in a special way at specific points in time and to specific people. "In many and various ways God spoke of old to our fathers by the prophets" (Heb 1:1). It is for this reason that revelation has been called within Christianity "the fundamental principle of theology and faith".[4] At the same time, when we speak about revelation as God's self-disclosure we do not thereby deny his ultimate incomprehensibility and the profound mystery of his being. The various formulations of dogmatic theology can be seen as protectors of the mystery of God against all attempts at rationalization.

> Only that which is given by the unsearchable freedom of love has power to reveal. And so analogously (the similarity is overruled by the greater dissimilarity!) the free self-disclosure of the divine heart sheds over all our existence, thought, loving

and action an incomparable light; and yet it comes from the God 'who dwells in unapproachable light, whom no man has ever seen or can see' (1 Tim 6:16). And yet we are to draw near to the inaccessible one 'in boldness and confidence through our faith in Jesus Christ' (Eph 3:12) who has 'expounded' to us the inaccessible God 'whom no man has seen' (Jn 1:18).[5]

The English word "revelation" comes from the Latin, "*revelare*", meaning "to take away the veil", to uncover that which was previously covered. Thus it includes the action of revealing and that which is revealed. It is different from discovery, in the sense that we discover something for ourselves while we reveal it to others. In Christianity this action of revealing is performed by God himself and it could only be so precisely because for Christians God is the absolutely inaccessible. As Jean Daniélou wrote some years ago: "The first article of the Christian faith is the doctrine of the Creator-God, that is, the radical distinction between God and man. Accordingly, God alone is able to raise man to this participation in him which is the supernatural life."[6] We can only know God if God chooses to make himself known. If we can know God through the contemplation of creatures, it is because he has freely chosen to reveal himself in this way. If we can perceive him in certain historical events and persons it is, again, because he has chosen to manifest himself in this manner. *What* he reveals is his plan or mystery which was conceived from all eternity and hidden in his own innermost being, a plan of salvation for all humanity, and it is this which forms the background, the inner dynamic core of revelation.[7]

Creation is the action which initiates this process. Paul puts it like this: "For what can be known about God is plain to them, because God has shown it to them. Ever since the creation of the world his invisible nature, namely, his eternal power and deity, has been clearly perceived in the things that have been made. So they are without excuse" (Rom 1:19–20). Thus in creation God reveals himself and since man is the highest aspect of this creation known to us then man himself is the highest aspect of this type of revelation. Through reflection on his own being and on the world about him man can achieve a certain, albeit limited and open to distortion, knowledge of God and of his will. This springs from the fact that the creature must necessarily in some way reveal its creator. This type of revelation is usually referred to as "natural" revelation although the adjective is not without its difficulties and a better name for it might be "anonymous" revelation.

Furthermore, it must be pointed out that we can only speak about revelation in this way because in Christianity God is conceived of as personal. The "absolute" as such, the "transcendent", cannot speak. Revelation can only be conceived as meaningful for us if God is first and foremost conceived as personal, capable of communicating, of entering into relationships, for, strictly speaking, revelation can only take place between two subjects, between two minds. There cannot be revelation between an object and a subject, for the simple reason that an object is incapable of *disclosing itself*, taking away the veil from its inner being, as it were. That can only happen between persons. Revelation, therefore, is between a Divine subject, God, and a human subject. Revelation, as understood within Christianity, is not the revelation of knowledge *about* God but the revelation *of* God, the *self*-disclosure of God.

Revelation, in the religious sense of the term, demands not only that God "speaks" to man but also that man can "hear" God. Humanity's being must have the capacity to be "open" to God, to be able to receive his revelation.

In the Catholic concept of revelation, a distinction is made between the form of revelation which human beings, contemplating their own natures and the world about them, can come to know by means of their reasoning powers and the revelation which God grants to them and which they, unaided, could never have achieved. This is usually referred to as "supernatural" revelation. It transcends the natural powers of the human being although the human being has the capacity to receive it. This second form of revelation comes to man not through the works of God in creation but through the word of God, spoken by God to humanity. This word of God was spoken in time, to chosen agents, but achieved its definitive and absolute form in the Son of God who is his Word in a special way. Jesus is God's Word in person. Natural revelation is sometimes said to be atemporal, in the sense that it is co-terminous with creation (although, to be revelation in the true sense, it can only take place in the historical encounter with a person or persons). Creation can be the vehicle by means of which God communicates himself but that communication requires the encounter with an historical subject if it is to take place. Supernatural revelation is, in a similar way, said to be temporal, in the sense that it took place at particular times within history. The distinction made here is not really acceptable, for it presupposes revelation as an object "something" rather than the self-disclosure, the self-communication, of God. Revelation, as we have said, is not so much the communication of truths about God's nature as the giving of himself in communion.

For that reason, it would be wrong to think of "natural" revelation as being in any way opposed to "supernatural" revelation. Both have to do with God's plan of salvation for the whole world and especially for every human being within that world. Both have their origin in God (and for that reason there is dissatisfaction with the term "natural" as it would seem to imply that it is not from God in the same way that "supernatural" revelation is). Supernatural revelation is necessary if man is to know the destiny to which God has called him. Mankind's vocation is one, divine.[8] It reveals to the human person the meaning of his or her existence here on earth and how he or she is to live out his or her life in order to achieve the destiny to which he or she is called. Because of supernatural revelation we now know that humanity has been created for God and that therefore the human heart cannot rest "until it rests in God". This truth is not something which we could discover by our own powers. We can indeed hear God's word, but that God would have chosen us to share his own life could never have been deduced by us from our existential situations. The ability to hear this special Word of God, to accept it and respond to it, is called faith and is itself a gift from God. We will discuss it more fully in the next chapter.

As Christians, it is our firm conviction that God has indeed revealed himself. This is our faith and it is from this standpoint that we examine the question. We seek to understand the faith that is in us and so we turn to the Bible which is for us the supreme attestation of God's revelation. We approach the Bible, not as the literal word of God but rather as a collection of religious writings stemming from different periods of Israel's long history, having many authors, and through this collection of writings we discover God's revelation. Through the many words, signs, of the Bible, God reveals himself and his plan for humanity. By means of the human words of Scripture God reveals his Word.

Revelation in the Old Testament

In the Old Testament, the Mysterious Being who eventually becomes known by the name Yahweh reveals himself not in any abstract terms but in revelatory actions, deeds, which were announced in his name and which took place as historical facts. It was announced to a particular group of people, the Israelites, that if they trust in this Being, this Power, then they would obtain freedom, liberation from slavery and be given a land of their own. In this way the people gradually came to know Yahweh, the One with them, to know him as a "person", to experience his power and his will for them. Thus did he reveal himself to them and so they entered into a relationship with him. He was their God and they were his people. It took many years before it was brought home to them that this Yahweh was not only their God but was the only God, no other God existing.

For the Israelites the supreme event of God's revelation, the supreme disclosure of his love for them, his will for them, was the event known as the Exodus, their liberation from the life of abject slavery in Egypt and their being led into the promised land of milk and honey. Thus they experienced Yahweh as their liberator, their redeemer. However, this was not the only event. When, because of their own infidelities, they were driven out of the Promised

Land, became exiles in Babylon and only after a number of years were able to return, only then did they begin to realize that the full revelation of Yahweh's love for them, his will, the full revelation of his power and glory, still lay in the future; indeed it would only take place at the end of time – it would be an eschatological event.

Thus revelation, as understood in the Old Testament, consists first of all in signs that take place at specific times and in specific locations. It is therefore historically conditioned, not something that is always and everywhere present. However, the event, the sign, is not without its word. The event is understood and interpreted through the prophets.

> It is in this word that God's saving act, accomplished in the historical fact itself, and his revelation of himself formally became for us revelation. God's saving activity – revelation in reality – and his word – revelation in word – are therefore indissolubly united to each in the one divine revelation. . . . The prophetic message threw light on the presence and the content of the saving act and, if the message preceded the events, even brought about the presence of a saving fact. It was precisely because salvation was revealed in a veiled manner in an event belonging strictly to this world, that is, in Jewish history, that the unerring recognition of the fact of salvation required the prophetic message. The word thus forms an integral part of the manifestation of God's saving activity.[9]

The word and the event are inextricably united. Thus revelation, this historical word/event, this sign which manifests something of God to man, is not a mere announcement but is a *creative* word, a word that brings about that which it signifies. In the light of this, revelation, as understood in the Bible, is not just a word *about* God, *about* grace, life and salvation but is a word that makes God present, a word that *is* itself grace, life and salvation. This means that the word of God, his *dabar*, is act. It is in this way that it proves itself and so his word is always a saving word.

This is not to say that it was always understood, perceived or accepted in this way. Humanity is free to accept or reject the word of God. Likewise, it is important to point out that the saving word/act of God is always something that is totally gratuitous, totally unmerited by man, and is something that springs from God's gracious freedom and love.

And so the inhabitants of ancient Israel entered into a relationship with God, not from the contemplation of nature but on account of the events of their own history even though the full significance of these events was not always perceived or accepted by those on whose behalf they took place. Later in their history, their apocalyptic writers tended to see the different historical actions of God as moments of one single history, a history that awaited its completion. The different words/events were aspects of the definitive word/event which still lay in the future. The revelation which is initiated in the Old Testament seeks its fulfilment in the New.

Revelation in the New Testament

Jesus Christ is the definitive Word/Event of God. In him all other words/events are subsumed and receive their definitive expression. For that reason Jesus Christ *is* the revelation of God, both as the action of revealing and the content of what is revealed. This revelation comes to its supreme expression in the paschal mystery. There, in the death and resurrection of Jesus, we find the most profound concentration of Christian revelation. Jesus is the "mystery", the *"sacramentum"* of God, hidden from all eternity, the plan of God "for the fulness of time, to unite all things in him, things in heaven and things on earth" (Eph 1:10). He is, indeed, the "Alpha and the Omega, the beginning and the end" (Rev 21:6). He is "the light of the world" (Jn 9:5) and in this light we can come to a knowledge of the truth of creation, come to a knowledge of God and of his plan for humanity. Jesus Christ is the criterion of revelation, seen as an action of unveiling and also as the contents which are thus unveiled. He is the unique Word of God existing from all eternity which is made present in the world. Edward Schillebeeckx put it like this:

Christ among us was, in and through his historically situated and conditioned humanity, the revelation of God. He was thus God's word — God himself, the Son, addressing us personally in the man Jesus. God the Son was a personal fellow-man who dealt with us as man to man, at the personal level. Every truly human act on Christ's part was, therefore, even more strongly than in the history of the Old Testament, a word spoken by God to man. Moreover, here the dialogue in the proper sense acquired its fullest significance. If Jesus' humanity was the medium of divine revelation, then this implies that Jesus' human word literally acquired a constitutive significance in this revelation.[10]

Revelation, therefore, in its most definitive form is Jesus Christ himself. In him God manifests himself to us in a personal, historical and totally grace-filled way.

The most fundamental aspect of the revelation made known through Jesus Christ is that God is love, that God is *communion*, that God is dynamic relationship. Through Jesus Christ we discover that the one God is Trinity, and this revelation is at the foundation of the Christian vision of the world, of its origin and destiny. When this is forgotten, then we cease to have a true *Christian* viewpoint. When we forget that the God who is revealed in Jesus Christ is the triune God then we can no longer claim to be speaking as Christians nor can we talk of what our relationship with other religions should or should not be. Indeed, as has been mentioned before, our relationship with other religions is of vital interest to us precisely because of the revelation of God as relationship, as love; and as Christians, our response to all peoples, whether they accept or reject Jesus Christ, can only be a response of love. As Christians, the supreme command of love must prevail and we must ever strive to bring about that universal brotherhood which is our specific mission. A Christian is one who believes that every human being, irrespective of race, creed or culture, is capable of being his or her brother or sister, worthy of being accepted, promoted, of being loved.

It is of the essence of Christian faith that in Jesus Christ revelation came to its completion. He is the one in whom the destiny of creation has already taken place. Even though history continues and the rest of us still await our fullness, our "maturity", our true "life" and wholeness, that fullness, that maturity, that life and wholeness has already been achieved in the risen Christ. In the life, death and resurrection of Jesus Christ we contemplate the finished product, the new creation, the new man, and in him we contemplate our own ultimate destiny, that in which we are invited to share. What Jesus now is, is what each one of us can aspire to become. United with him we can hope to share his life, his happiness. In the risen Lord we see the fullness of the power and the glory of God, we see his love. The resurrection of Jesus is the one, unique revelation of God himself, a God who is infinite, eternal, personal communion and love. The one God who is Father, Son and Holy Spirit is the God who is revealed in Jesus Christ. It is only in this context that we can truly talk of revelation.

The God who is revealed in Jesus Christ is the same God who is revealed in creation but it is because of the life, death and resurrection of Jesus Christ that this is fully understood. From one point of view, creation can be seen as the ungodly, the non-divine − in the sense that creation is not God, the creature is distinct from its Creator. However, from another point of view, creation is precisely the medium through which God chose to reveal himself. Creation is, as it were, the recipient of God's self-revelation and is, therefore, so constituted that it is capable of receiving this gift of God himself, a capacity that finds its supreme and definitive expression in the man Jesus whose humanity becomes in a special way the "vehicle" of the divinity to such an extent that he is the God-man. But by reason of this very fact − that he is the God-man − all creation becomes in a limited and partial sense a means by which God reveals himself to us. Of course, without the fullness of revelation in Christ we would be unable to know that it is the revelation of God to us or the sense in which it is the revelation of God to us.

Revelation outside of Christianity

When we come to the question, therefore, of whether revelation is to be found outside of Christianity or not, a number of points have to be kept in mind. The first is that man can, even apart from contact with the revelation that is found in the Judaeo-Christian context, come to a certain, limited knowledge of God. By means of natural reason and the observation of the physical world in which he lives, he can arrive at the concept of God that is omnipotent, intelligent, personal — he can even arrive, it would seem, at the concept of a creator God who maintains in existence the world he has created. By means of his own conscience, man can come to a knowledge of God as the source of our moral obligations, the one who will reward our good conduct and punish us if we do evil. By looking into the depths of his own being, man can come to know God as the ultimate ground of his spirit. In this way, without any reference to Scripture, human beings are capable of arriving at quite an extensive knowledge of God and of his attributes and through this knowledge enter into a certain relationship with God. However, despite what we have said, Barth was right when he wrote that to claim that man could know God by the unaided human reason "is an outrage upon the Christian idea of God",[11] because it is not quite correct to speak of man arriving at such a knowledge, entering into such a relationship, unaided, by means of reason alone. We know that in the world that God has created there always exists a supernatural dimension to man's being. God, right from the beginning, has destined man to share his own life. Humanity, by creation, is God-oriented and therefore his "natural" existence is always a *graced* existence. As Rahner has brought out, grace is always present at the very heart of man's existence, at least in the "mode of an offer", grace which can either be accepted or rejected.

However indisputable it may be that grace in its intrinsic nature can also have effects in the individual phenomena of the consciousness, still grace as such must be understood as an element of the actual transcendentality of human beings by means of which they are always and of necessity open to the absolute reality of God. . . Thus grace, even though it is of course unmerited, can, because of God's universal salvific will, always and everywhere be present, at least in the mode of an offer, even if it remains entirely open whether this grace will be accepted or rejected by human freedom. . . This radical ordination and this radicalizing of human transcendentality to the immediacy of God, even though it is not the object of explicit reflection and verbalization, can be quite rightly understood as "revelation". For it is gratuitous, whereby the "gratuitous character" must not be confused with the idea of a gift that is fine or exclusive because it is rare or with an endowment which is bestowed at a definite point in place and time, both of which are conceivable but do not belong to the essence of an unmerited grace. This radicalizing of human transcendentality to the immediacy of God can further be understood as revelation because it gives to knowledge and freedom a new, otherwise unattainable formal object. It is a personal revelation of God because it is given through God's free, personal self-communication, which constitutes the actual essence of grace. This revelation can be quite properly understood as fundamentally historical (despite the criticism of Eicher and others) because it is obvious that every transcendental human experience is always mediated by a historical experience and forms a unity with it.[12]

This grace is indeed supernatural grace, nothing less than God himself, dwelling at the very centre of man's existence. It is an ontological aspect of man's being, determining it in a specific way, enabling him to experience the transcendental quality which is distinctive of man's experience of God.

However, lest we become over-enthused about the extent of man's "natural" knowledge of God and the relationship thereby created, it is important to remember that graced man is at one and the same time fallen man, immersed in a situation of sin, a situation that alienates him from his true destiny and frustrates his efforts to attain it. Sin, while not destroying people's capacity to desire their true end, has rendered them incapable of achieving it. This alienation of the human person has made humanity's knowledge of God to be subject to error and distortion. Indeed, some would claim that the knowledge of God that man can attain from within his sinful situation is so debased that it cannot be called true knowledge of God at all. St Paul himself, in his Letter to the Romans, would seem to imply as much when he writes:

> For what can be known about God is plain to them, because God has shown it to them. Ever since the creation of the world his invisible nature, namely, his eternal power and deity, has been clearly perceived in the things that have been made. So they are without excuse: for although they knew God they did not honour him as God or give thanks to him, but they became futile in their thinking and their senseless minds were darkened. Claiming to be wise, they became fools, and exchanged the glory of the immortal God for images resembling mortal man or birds or animals or reptiles.
>
> Therefore God gave them up in the lusts of their hearts to impurity, to the dishonouring of their bodies among themselves, because they exchanged the truth about God for a lie and worshipped and served the creature rather then the Creator, who is blessed for ever! Amen. (Rom 1:19–25).

On its face value this passage would seem to deny all real knowledge of God outside the Judaeo-Christian world.[13] However, let it not be forgotten to whom the Letter is addressed, and that what Paul had in mind was his contemporary Graeco-Roman world. Likewise, we must remember that it is the same Paul who addressed the Athenians at the Areopagus and recognized that "what, therefore, you worship as unknown, this I proclaim to you" (Acts 17:23). It would seem strange if God, who has called each and every human being to share in his own eternal life, should have allowed all vestiges of true knowledge of himself to be destroyed in the hearts of men and women, except for those within the tiny Judaeo-Christian enclave! On the contrary, experience would seem to indicate that there is indeed a true knowledge of God to be found among the nations, albeit in a limited and obscure form.

From historical experience we know of the existence of

religious "geniuses" — men and women endowed with a highly developed sense of the sacred, accompanied by deep insights into human nature and destiny. In the insights of such people many more came to recognize as acceptable and worthy of credence the explanations thus afforded to the deepest questions of human beings, their origin, destiny, problems, etc. As we have stressed so often, man is by nature a social being, created to live in society, and this affects all his relationships. "No man is an island", said John Donne and few would dispute it. And, as Vatican II pointed out, "unless (man) relates himself to others, he can neither live nor develop his potential."[14] And the same Council declared elsewhere: "It has pleased God, however, to make men holy and save them not merely as individuals without any mutual bonds but by making them into a single people, a people which acknowledges him in truth and serves him in holiness."[15] Religion is the normal way in which man expresses his basic orientation towards God. Therefore, it is a justified assumption that the true knowledge of God and man's relationship to him, even when this is found with a greater or lesser degree of error due to man's fallen nature, should find expression in the different religions of the people. To the extent that true knowledge of God is to be found in the different religions, there is true relationship with him and therefore true salvation. I would therefore conclude that there is true salvation to be found outside the Christian world and that this salvation is mediated through the different religions.

Nevertheless, for a Christian it is only the fullness of revelation as found in Christ that can authenticate this revelation. Only the light of the Gospel can show its truth as also its error. This does not mean the light of a historical manifestation of the Gospel. Indeed, each particular manifestation must itself be in a continual state of examination as to its fidelity to Christ, the Gospel Message. Conversion, *metanoia*, is a permanent feature of Christianity here on earth. If revelation is seen as God revealing himself to man, speaking to him, teaching him, trying to win his fidelity, opening up to man his vocation in life, his destiny, the reason for which he has been created, God's plan for him, and if this process of revelation is experienced by man as responding to his deepest desires, his most profound longings, then it is right to ask if there is any way whereby we can know if such a revelation has indeed taken place. Jesus once gave a very simple criterion of truth: "You will know them by their fruits" (Mt 7:16). And since the fruit of revelation is communion with God, entry into his life, which is a life of infinite love, then surely the only criterion of the presence of revelation, authentic revelation, has to be the presence of authentic love. Another way of putting it is that the fruit of true revelation is the gift of the Spirit of God, the Spirit which is the bond of union between the Father and the Son. Scripture tells us that "where the Spirit of the Lord is, there is freedom" (2 Cor 3:17) and what the Spirit brings is "love, joy, peace, patience, kindness, goodness, faithfulness, gentleness, self-control" (Gal 5:22).

Each religion, including Christianity as a religion, must be examined to see in what measure it promotes these qualities in the lives of its followers. *A priori* one cannot say that this or that religion contains true revelation or not; that can only be said after a thorough examination of the particular religion. What I feel can be said, however, is that *a priori* there is no reason why they should not contain true revelation and in the measure in which they do they can mediate salvation for their adherents. It would seem probable that the great religions of the world — those that have won the fidelity of millions of people through thousands of years — do contain true revelation and are, therefore, salvific.

However, revelation is the communication of truth and this involves what has been called teaching or doctrine. This is precisely the area where people will dispute the presence of revelation in the other religions. In the past, this aspect of revelation predominated to such an extent that it was often thought to be the only element of revelation. Today, with the emphasis on revelation as relationship, as communion, teaching has taken a somewhat less prominent role.

This was inevitable; yet, if revelation is seen as God entering into a relationship with man, it must not be forgotten that man is an intelligent being and needs teaching about God so that he can enter into a meaningful relationship with him. For this reason, the teaching of other religions must be examined. And here again, *a priori* we cannot say that it is true or false without first making a thorough examination using Jesus Christ as our criterion of judgement.

One of the big criticisms against Christian revelation is the fact that it is linked to specific historical events. Because of this, some would suggest that in order to be relevant in our modern world these events must be "mythologized", for only in that way can they break the limiting bonds of history and become of universal significance. Against this it must be remembered that historicity belongs to the very essence of the human condition and if God is going to encounter us as humans then this must take place historically, and the very fact that we proclaim the historicity of revelation, far from being a limitation, it rather underlines its fundamental relevance for us as historical beings. To "mythologize" it, dehistoricize it, would be to empty it of any real meaning for us. This historical element is found also in non-Christian religions, in the sense that what leads men to convictions concerning God are usually experiences of his working in the historical events of their lives.

One of the noticeable features of biblical revelation is its universal dimensions — found throughout the whole Bible. I have already referred to the fact that in the Old Testament, we find it in the covenant made with Noah which involved the whole of creation. Indeed, the first twelve chapters of Genesis are vitally important for an understanding of our relationship with other religions. Creation itself can be seen as a covenant made between God and the world he has brought into being. Every man and woman is "Adam" — a human being. God calls each by name, and there is no human being on earth nor any human community living outside this covenant. The fact that a human being has been called into existence is proof of the fact that that person has been called by God to share with him eternal

life. This "covenant of creation" is the presupposition, and
also the anticipation, of all future covenants — that of
Abraham, that of Sinai and that of Christ, "the new and
everlasting covenant". The other covenants confirm and
bring to its fullness this initial, opening covenant. One could
trace this universal dimension of revelation right through
the patriarchs from Abraham, in whom "all the families
of the earth shall bless themselves" (Gen 12:3) and who
himself was blessed by the pagan priest, Melchizedek (Gen
14:20). In the vocation of Abraham we see that the people
of Israel are called to render a service of reconciliation and
reunion for all peoples. Israel was often tempted to see itself
as the chosen of the Lord to the exclusion of other people,
to forget its role of service and to constitute itself as a club
for "members only". Over and over again the prophets
strive to keep the universalist orientation alive and make
the people realize that their election does not imply a special
privilege:

> "Are you not like the Ethiopians to me,
> O people of Israel?" says the Lord.
> "Did I not bring up Israel from the land of Egypt,
>   and the Philistines from Caphtor
>   and the Syrians from Kir?" (Amos 9:7)

Isaiah proclaims that Yahweh "shall judge between the
nations, and shall decide for many peoples" (2:4). Jeremiah
feels himself sent not only to Israel but also appointed by
the Lord as "a prophet to the nations" (1:5). The Lord said
to him: "See, I have set you this day over nations and over
kingdoms" (1:10). The crisis of the Exile tested their faith
in Yahweh and they became aware of their own rebellious-
ness, disobedience and infidelity (Ez 16; 20:5-26:21). God
is going to purify Israel so that it will fulfil the covenant,
and in this way fulfil its mission to the Gentiles, and "they
will know that I am the Lord God" (Ez 29:16). Little by
little the mysterious figure of the Suffering Servant of
Yahweh makes his appearance. His mission is not limited
to gathering together the dispersed sons of Israel — it has
a universal horizon:

It is too light a thing that you should be my servant to raise up the tribes of Jacob and to restore the preserved of Israel; I will give you as a light to the nations, that my salvation may reach to the ends of the earth. (Is 49:6)

In the post-exilic period Israel tended once again to close in on itself but the universalism does not entirely disappear, summed up by the prophet Malachi in these beautiful words:

For from the rising of the sun to its setting my name is great among the nations, and in every place incense is offered to my name, and a pure offering; for my name is great among the nations, says the Lord of hosts. (1:11)

The final words of the Book of Jonah underline the fact that the mercy of God has no frontiers:

And should not I pity Nineveh, that great city, in which there are more than a hundred and twenty thousand persons who do not know their right hand from their left, and also much cattle? (4:11)

The authors of the Wisdom Books are also aware of this universalist dimension of their faith in Yahweh. They remind Israel that creation itself reveals God: "For from the greatness and beauty of created things comes a corresponding perception of their Creator" (Wis 13:5). In the great hymns of Proverbs 8, Job 28 and Sirach 24, creation is presented as the cosmic voice which reveals God and the hearers of this voice are not merely the Israelites but the inhabitants of the whole world. God himself makes man capable of seeing the greatness of God's works and of leading a life in conformity with his will:

He made for them tongue and eyes;
    he gave them ears and a mind for thinking.
He filled them with knowledge and understanding,
    and showed them good and evil.
He set his eye upon their hearts
    to show them the majesty of his works.
And they will praise his holy name,
    to proclaim the grandeur of his works.
He bestowed knowledge upon them,
    and allotted to them the law of life.

He established with them an eternal covenant,
  and showed them his judgments.
Their eyes saw his glorious majesty,
  and their ears heard the glory of his voice.
And he said to them, "Beware of all unrighteousness."
  And he gave commandment to each of them
    concerning his neighbour. (Sir 17:6–14)

So in the Old Testament we discover a universal line going right through the history of Israel even though we also find Israel's constant temptation to constitute itself a club and to make Yahweh a merely tribal God. They saw in their election as the People of God a privilege to be defended rather than a task to be performed.

It was into this environment that Jesus was born and from an examination of his teaching on the kingdom of God and of the image of God which he projected — God as the one who invites all mankind, as the one who always receives, always forgives — it was very clear to the early Church that his message and his mission were for the whole world not just for Israel. Because of Christ all barriers have been broken down and "there is neither Jew nor Greek, there is neither slave nor free, there is neither male nor female; for you are all one in Christ Jesus" (Gal 3:28). He relativizes the importance of belonging to a particular race or social class and instead emphasizes the importance of sincerity and authenticity. God, he insists, is to be worshipped in spirit and in truth. God has certainly revealed himself in a special way through Israel and above all through Jesus, a revelation that is continued through his Church — but this does not mean that his Spirit, his truth, is confined. By his life and teaching, Christ attacked all exclusivism, underlining that it was the poor, the marginalized, the strangers, who would first enter the kingdom of heaven. I will leave further discussion of this topic to the chapter on Mission. Suffice it to say that God's revelatory Word is not tied, for his Spirit "blows where it wills" (Jn 3:8).

NOTES

1. Werner Bulst, *Revelation* (Sheed & Ward, New York 1965), p. 82.
2. Ronald F. Thiemann, *Revelation and Theology. The Gospel as Narrated Promise* (University of Notre Dame Press, Notre Dame, Indiana 1987), p. 1.
3. Of the many books available today on the subject of Revelation the following are of particular interest: Avery Dulles, *Models of Revelation* (Image Books, Garden City, N.Y. 1985); Gabriel Moran, *The Theology of Revelation* (Herder and Herder, New York 1966); Gabriel Moran, *The Present Revelation* (Herder and Herder, New York 1972); René Latourelle, *Theology of Revelation*, (Alba House, Staten Island, N.Y. 1966); Gerard O'Collins, *Foundations of Theology* (Loyola University Press, Chicago 1966); Aylward Shorter, *Revelation* (Geoffrey Chapman, London 1983); Edward Schillebeeckx, *Revelation and Theology* Vol. 1 (Sheed & Ward, London 1967, 1987); Hans-Urs von Balthasar, *Word and Revelation* (Herder and Herder, New York 1964); Heinrich Fries, *Revelation* (Burns and Oates, London and Herder and Herder, New York 1970).
4. Heinrich Fries, *Revelation*, p. 17.
5. Hans-Urs von Balthasar, *Elucidations* (SPCK, London 1975), p. 24.
6. Jean Daniélou, "The Transcendence of Christianity", in J. Daniélou et al. *Great Religions* (Fides Publishers Inc., Notre Dame, Indiana 1964), p. 137.
7. E. Schillebeeckx, *Revelation and Theology* Vol. 1, pp. 2–11.
8. Cf. Vatican II: *Gaudium et Spes*, 22.
9. E. Schillebeeckx, *Revelation and Theology* Vol. 1, p. 9; see also pp. 36–62.
10. *Ibid.,* pp. 40–41.
11. Karl Barth, *Church Dogmatics* II, 1 (T & T Clark, Edinburgh 1956), p. 40.
12. Karl Rahner, "The Act of Faith and the Content of Faith", *Theological Investigations* Vol XXI (Darton, Longman and Todd, London and Seabury Press, New York 1988), pp. 156–157.
13. Barth would thus interpret the passage; cf. *Church Dogmatics* 1/2, pp. 280–354.
14. *Gaudium et Spes*, 12.
15. *Lumen Gentium*, 9.

4

Faith

In the last chapter we saw how revelation is the Mystery of God made known to man. God, in his infinite freedom, has chosen to manifest himself through signs to mankind, to communicate *himself* – and thereby salvation. This process began with creation and culminated in the life, death and resurrection of Jesus Christ. He is the Sign of signs. In him, God has promised *everything*, has communicated *himself*, and therefore no further revelation is expected nor can be expected. That is why Christianity cannot be surpassed.[1] We saw how the structure of revelation is both Trinitarian and incarnational. In it, God the Father reveals himself as communion, God communicating himself infinitely and perfectly to his Son in the Spirit – and this life of communion is the one God. Through creation God has chosen to invite humanity to enter into his own happiness, to enter into a relationship with him. The God who is communion manifested his nature in Jesus Christ. Revelation became incarnate in him. Revelation is for that reason nothing less than the *self-communication* of God and as such it is wholly supernatural, effected in the power of the Holy Spirit. From man's point of view, revelation is the making known of salvation. We saw that the two cannot be separated and, like revelation, salvation is also wholly supernatural, something that is brought about in and through the Spirit of God. However, revelation and salvation, if they are to be such, demand someone to receive them. They are not simply objective realities, something out there waiting, as it were, to be grasped. They are not independent data. Unreceived revelation, like unreceived salvation, is a contradiction in terms. In this connection, we are reminded of the words of our Lord: "Blessed are you, Simon Bar-Jona! For flesh and blood has not revealed this to you, but my

Father in heaven" (Mt 16:17). God is the revealer, the
saviour, and the action by means of which we are
capacitated to respond to him as such we call faith.

Faith as a response

Faith[2] is the response of man to the self-communication
of God in Jesus Christ, a response that is carried out in and
through the power of the Holy Spirit. Christian faith is
always belief in Someone first and foremost, and if I believe
in something, it is precisely because I believe in Someone.
It is the means by which we appropriate to ourselves the
Mystery of God and, like revelation and salvation, it springs
totally from God's initiative, from his infinite goodness,
from God's graciousness. The capacity to receive God's
revelation as well as the actual reception of that revelation
comes from God. It is grace. It is nothing less than God
himself, for the Word of God can be apprehended only by
the power of God, the power of his Spirit. Thus revelation
and faith are the two sides of the one coin, two aspects of
the one saving encounter with God, an encounter in which
God retains the initiative in all aspects and yet man is not
thereby annulled. "Faith presupposes my personal decision.
If it could be proved, it would no longer be faith."[3] The
whole process is grace-filled, yet grace is not destructive of
man's freedom, of man's nature, but rather reveals their
full extent, for it includes their ultimate destiny, their most
fundamental orientation.

The concept "faith" is a complex one, susceptible of
many definitions, as is evidenced by the different uses of
the word that have been made down through the centuries
and in our own time. The word has been used to refer to
the foundation of all human knowledge as also to the
action by means of which an object of knowledge is
apprehended by the human mind; it has been used to
explain man's imaginative capacity as well as the foundation of the interpersonal relationships between two friends.
In the religious context, it expresses man's knowledge of
the divinity as well as his manner of relating to it. In

Christianity, the word "faith" has been reserved for that encounter with God which comes about through the revelatory signs which are to be found in the history of salvation. Thus, we do not normally apply the word "faith" to that encounter with God which is mediated through his creation. This is usually called "natural" knowledge of God. I will return to this point later. For the moment, since I have said that faith is the encounter of man with God's saving revelation of himself in Jesus Christ, it is important to look briefly at our understanding of man. This is necessary because, to a certain extent at least, it is true what Pannenberg has said: "the whole burden of proof of the truth of faith in God falls upon the understanding of man, upon anthropology."[4]

In Western culture we have become accustomed to think of man in Aristotelian terms as being first and foremost "a rational animal". This was the definition accepted by Thomas Aquinas[5] and it has so influenced our thought that very often the rational dimension of man has practically excluded all other dimensions of his being. It influenced St Thomas in his treatment of the faith and although he himself was able to maintain the unity of faith with the other dimensions of Christian life many of his followers were not, so that faith came to be presented in almost exclusively intellectual terms (at least within the Catholic tradition, while within Protestantism the volitional aspect of faith was stressed). For many Catholics, faith came to be understood as above all the giving of intellectual assent to a set of doctrines, truths or dogmatic formulae. The Creed was something to be recited rather than lived. This understanding of faith was reinforced by Vatican I with its emphasis on the content of faith, the *fides quae*, the revealed truths.[6] This not infrequently led to a dichotomy between faith and life.

The biblical dimension of faith

The biblical and patristic understanding of faith is that of a personal encounter with the saving God as revealed in salvation history but above all as revealed in Jesus Christ, an encounter that demanded conversion, a personal decision to follow Christ, to discipleship. With the renewal of biblical and patristic studies this original understanding of faith has been rediscovered. Once again it is stressed that faith is a divine gift which establishes a special relationship between God and a human being in all his or her totality, as an individual, as a social being, as part of creation. It is at one and the same time a gift from God and a truly human act.

One of the important biblical rediscoveries of our century is that man is a unity, as opposed to the dualism found in Plato and practically all subsequent Western philosophers. For the Bible authors, man is above all a created being totally dependent on God for his existence and for his continuance here on earth. For them, faith was above all trust and confidence in this God who has created them, who is powerful in word and deed, who has revealed himself as a God radically committed to man, to his happiness and well-being. This is the whole point of creation, the very reason for its existence. For the people of the Old Testament this faith was made concrete in the acceptance and living out of the covenant with Yahweh.

This biblical understanding of man has been complemented in modern times by the studies of philosophers and anthropologists. Hegel and Marx underlined the fact that man is a social being, a being radically conditioned by history. He finds himself only by entering into relationships with others. Kierkegaard and the later existentialists stressed man's individuality but whose individuality can only find itself in social relationships. Because of this there is in the Church and in the world today a much more wholistic understanding of man than prevailed in some previous centuries.

Nevertheless, for us Christians, a central point is that God's commitment to mankind achieved its fullest expression in the Incarnation, the Word of God made man in Jesus Christ. Only in him therefore do we find a full anthropology, for only in him do we find the full, mature, realized man, willed by God. In him we find revealed not only God and his plan for creation, we also find revealed man, his origin, his destiny. In Jesus we have the new Man, the new Adam, saved humanity. In the risen Lord[7] we have the perfect expression of God's invitation to man to enter into communion with himself and likewise we have the perfect response on the part of man to that invitation. Christ *is* at one and the same time the invitation offered to mankind by God and the invitation accepted by mankind. In him, revelation, the response to it (faith) and salvation find their perfect, complete and definitive expression.

For that reason, we have to look at Christ in order to understand what faith really means. Through him we discover that it is fully the work of the Holy Spirit. It is the Spirit in us that enables us to make our response to God, to accept our creaturehood, our total dependence on the God who has called us to life and who maintains that life in existence. It is the Spirit that enables us to call out "Abba! Father!" (Rom 8:15). Without the power of the Holy Spirit, faith, understood as a response to God's self-communication, is impossible. Cardinal Newman summed it up nicely when he wrote: "We believe, because we love." We do not believe against our wills. We do not believe God because what he says is interesting, intelligent, important or even because it is true but because the Spirit gives us the grace to do so. The Spirit existing within the Godhead is, as it were, the animating force of its communion and it is only through him that we can enter into it, share in the communion. Saving faith is therefore the work of the Holy Spirit; he is the "soul of the entire ecclesiastical community of faith"[8], he who brings about any saving faith in the world. Through him we are enabled to recognize that all that we are and have come from God and that of ourselves we are nothing. We know from revelation that the God who has created us is a good God, a God who loves us, who is all powerful and who has called each and every human being to share his life. Faith gives man "a part in the communion of saints, a fellowship transcending the bounds of time and space."[9] Faith is precisely the trusting in his care and love for us; it is the abandoning of ourselves to his plan for us; it is the acceptance of him as our creator, our Lord and our God. It is this faith, this trusting attitude, that is the ground of our gratitude, our confidence, our hope and our love. They are all aspects of the one reality, the one response here on earth to our God. While we journey in this world, this response is subject to the law of history, to the law of temporality, and from that point of view it is not certain – our response can be changed or revoked at any time. But from the point of view of the *object* of our trust, of our confidence, it is solid as a rock, for God's fidelity is immovable, unchangeable. Grace does not destroy our freedom, it liberates it to be truly freedom, to be free for God. But because we are sinners we can also misuse our freedom, reject the Lord's invitation, refuse to enter into the communion, the relationship to which we are invited. While faith is the work of the Spirit in us, it is also the action of human beings.

> Faith is a compact act of many different aspects. No doubt these may be analysed, but they form an organic whole and are therefore unintelligible unless studied in their organic interrelation. Modern exegetes are agreed that faith includes knowledge of a saving event, confidence in the word of God, man's humble submission and personal self-surrender to God, fellowship in life with Christ and a desire for perfect union with him beyond the grave: faith is man's comprehensive "Yes" to God revealing himself as man's saviour in Christ.[10]

It is indeed man who believes, and while all is grace, man, as I have said, is not displaced by grace. God calls us as human beings and this means that he calls us in our fullness, taking into account the fact that we are socially oriented individuals and that our fullness is yet to come. Our faith is a personal response to God made in our encounter with Jesus Christ. Apart from him, no response is possible, no faith is possible, just as apart from him there is no salvation and no revelation in the true sense of the word. Man only makes a true act of faith when he unites himself to Jesus Christ. In this way he responds to God's self-communication. Here we cannot go into the complex question of the relationship of grace and freedom. Nevertheless, to help us to see faith within the contexts of both grace and freedom, reflection on the nature of personal encounters can be very helpful.

In a loving personal encounter, the lover calls for a response from the beloved and the beloved must respond in his or her freedom, yet it is the love of the lover that makes the response possible. In an analogous way, God calls us as individuals and we respond to him, yet it is he who makes our response possible. Our decision is based on knowledge, the knowledge that comes to us from revelation; but this knowledge is primarily the knowledge that exists between two lovers, it is a personal knowledge between two subjects rather than the knowledge which a subject acquires of an object. Where love is present, the slightest sign is sufficient to recognize the presence of the beloved.

Because Jesus is God's revelation, faith takes place in the personal encounter with him. In Christ, we meet the Revealer and the Revealed. Jesus Christ is the Word of God made man but it must never be forgotten that he is the Word of the *Triune* God, of the God who is communion, and, furthermore, our encounter with him is also an encounter with his communitarian dimension, with the whole Christ, head and members. Our response to him is therefore an encounter with the Church and made from within the Church, the Body of Christ. It is faith that brings us to the Church, that makes us members of the Church. The Church is primarily the communitarian dimension of our faith − a dimension that is prior to the individual dimension. It is the Church which offers the conditions for faith to be born in us, which enables us to make the response to God, for the Church is the "Mother of the faith" in the sense that the individual comes to the faith in and through the Church. The faith of each individual presupposes the community of faith and the individual can only live his or her faith from the faith of the community. There is only one faith and this unity stems from the unity of Christ to whom we are united in the faith. As Paul points out, Christ lives in our hearts "through faith" (Eph 3:17). In Christ is found the perfection of faith, as also the perfection of hope and love, a perfection to which we, as members of him, are called.

This brings us to the point that our faith is a faith that still awaits its perfection. Faith looks to its perfection in glory. It is eschatologically oriented and every aspect of the community of believers is likewise awaiting the "return of the Lord".

Christian faith, therefore, is the work of the Holy Spirit operative within the heart of man, uniting us with Christ, as individuals, as members of the Church, and awaiting its fullness when he returns. Through this union with Christ we are led to the Father, led to communion with the God of all things, and this communion is salvation. Faith is at once insertion into the reality of the Trinity and into the reality of the Incarnation. The two cannot be separated. From one point of view, we can say that all faith is centred on the Incarnation, for in the mystery of the Incarnation we find the mystery of the Trinity.

Faith outside the Church

And so we repeat our question. How is this faith, without which there is no salvation, to be predicated of those who have never heard of Christ? If, apart from Christ, there is no other way to the Father, "no one comes to the Father, but by me," (Jn 14:6), no other way to God, then it would seem that the majority of humanity are excluded from salvation. However, before coming to that conclusion, it is necessary to look again at Christ, the centre upon which the whole question turns.[11]

It is, as has been so often here repeated, the essence of our faith that God has communicated himself in Jesus Christ, that salvation can only be attained through him. It is likewise of the essence of our faith that Jesus Christ is true God and true man. Now, as man, Jesus is subject to all the conditions and limitations of what being human signifies. He is thus limited by space and time. Historically, Jesus was born in a little village in Palestine some two thousand years ago and he died on a hillside outside

Jerusalem some thirty-three years later and was then raised from the dead (although this later event is not understood in the same way historically as the preceding events). From one point of view, the only way mankind has of entering into a personal relationship with him is to have shared his earthly existence. However, because through faith we hold that this man was the Son of God, then it follows that his saving actions were the actions of God and as such were outside the bounds of space and time.[12] The process of responding to God's self-communication, from the point of view of humanity, is a process that began with the dawn of creation and will come to its fullness when Christ will have gathered to himself all his members. As was stressed elsewhere, creation and Incarnation must not be separated.[13] In this way we meet again the paradoxical oscillation between the "already" and the "not yet". The two are not opposed to each other but rather compenetrate each other in a creative, life-giving tension – a tension which has already been referred to and which lies at the heart of Christianity. Emphasizing one aspect at the expense of the other leads inevitably to falsification of the reality. So, from the very beginning of time, we find the Word present: "He was in the beginning with God; all things were made through him, and without him was not anything made that was made. In him was life, and the life was the light of men" (Jn 1:2–4). He is "the beginning of God's creation" (Rev 3:14). Thus we can say that faith, as a response to God through the Son in the Spirit, has been possible from the dawn of creation. All knowledge of the Father is through the Son. "He who has seen me has seen the Father" (Jn 14:9). This is not to extend the Church or explicit faith to include all history and all humanity within its boundaries – such would be to destroy its historicity, its humanness – but it does mean that the reality of God is added to this historicity; it is to recognize the transcendent within the historical. Jesus as man himself, in his deepest core as man, can transcend his own being, can, as it were, move out of himself into the infinite, so likewise this historicity of the faith, of the Church, does not negate its transcendence.[14]

Sometimes this faith found outside the Church, or even within the visible boundaries of the Church, is called "implicit" faith. In this way it was hoped to overcome the dilemma of the salvation of millions who seemingly do not have faith in Christ and who nevertheless seem to be living a better life than many who do profess such a faith. There are, however, good arguments against the term "implicit" faith, for it would seem to imply that faith has its roots in human consciousness as well as identifying the response of faith with the appreciation of certain human values. Too often one finds a confusion of faith with the sense of the sacred. This is indeed something human, something that does have its roots in human consciousness. In fact, this sense of the sacred can even have the trappings of Christian faith without being true Christian faith just as there can be a full consciousness of all the contents of faith without there being true faith at all. The problem with saying that non-Christians are saved by their "implicit" faith is that this fails to distinguish what is the ultimate significance of faith, as well as its practical consequences in this life, and the motivations which lie behind it.

As we have seen, true faith is the free, graced response to the gift of God himself; it is the adhesion of the whole person – intellect, will, emotions – to his Word, present at the very heart of creation and of humanity. Thus faith is not simply the discovery of human values, their fulfilment and explicitation. To live human values is not the same as living the faith although this latter does imply the profound and committed assumption of truly human values, the involvment in man's search for a better world. True Christian faith is to discover that only the covenant, the alliance of God with humanity brought about in Jesus Christ, can signify the fulfilment of man, can imply his salvation. From this it follows that if non-Christians are saved, if they are not to be irretrievably lost, then in some way they have to be united with us in the faith that we profess. Consequently they must be touched by grace; the Holy Spirit must have prepared them to live in the light of Jesus Christ. On this point Karl Rahner writes:

Christ is present and active in non-Christian believers (and therefore in non-Christian religions) through his Spirit. Such a statement is dogmatically self-evident. If salvific faith can be found in non-Christians and in fact may be expected to be found in them to a great extent, then it is self-evident that such a faith is made possible and is sustained by the supernatural grace of the Holy Spirit. And this is the Spirit who proceeds from the Father and the Son, so that as the Spirit of the eternal logos he can and must be called, at least in this sense, the Spirit of Christ, the Word of God became man.[15]

So that rather than speaking of "implicit" faith, we might speak of "embryonic" or "essential" faith, that faith which the Letter to the Hebrews demands as necessary for salvation: "And without faith it is impossible to please him. For whoever would draw near to God must believe that he exists and that he rewards those who seek him" (11:6). It is, however, the one faith in the sense that both — explicit, professed faith in Jesus Christ and essential, unprofessed faith in Christ — are a response to the revelation of God in Christ.

Karl Rahner has written an interesting essay on faith that can help us in this situation.[16] In it, he calls on the distinction between the *act* of faith, the "*fides qua*", and the *content* of faith, the "*fides quae*". The *fides qua* is the same everywhere but, obviously, the *fides quae* differs greatly from one person to another, even within the members of the Church. He writes:

There is a *fides qua* which exists as something that is a possibility for every human being (albeit something that is offered to a person's freedom) and which makes its significance for salvation and justification understandable through itself, and yet at the same time this *fides qua* possesses a reality of content in its own right, the free acceptance of which can be acknowledged as the acceptance of revelation in faith.[17]

As regards the content of faith, he goes on to say:

The *fides quae* may be quite minimal in content; in certain circumstances (as mediation of the free acceptance of grace) it can consist of that fidelity to one's own conscience in which, according to Vatican II, even persons who in a reflexive way

consider themselves to be atheists can still be in union with
the salvific mystery of Christ.[18]

Some may well ask: how can those who specifically
reject Jesus Christ have faith in the revelation which God
made through him? Is it not arrogant on the part of Christians
to impute to another that which the other professedly rejects?
In order to respond to these questions, I think it is important
to consider some points. First of all, it is impossible to impute
to *anybody* the presence or absence of saving faith. That is
caught up in the Mystery of God. As Christians we hope that
we have indeed entered into communion with our saving God,
and our hope is well founded but it is not scientific certitude
precisely because we are temporal and therefore subject to the
possibility of changing our commitment to God. This applies
to Christians as well as non-Christians. Faith, as outlined
above, is a gift from God, not something that we ourselves can
lay hold of, that we have a right to, that we can merit. The
living relationship with God which faith brings about is
initiated and established by God, not by ourselves. This
demands that when we come to impute the presence or absence
of faith, then we must be always conscious of our obligation
to respect God's liberty. We cannot judge what God does in
the consciences of individuals. Only God "searches all hearts
and understands every plan and thought" (1 Chron 28:9). We
know that he is a loving God, for thus he has revealed himself,
and that therefore he grants to each one what is necessary to
reach him. We do not know when he does this, under what
forms he does it or on what level of conduct. Here on earth
it is not up to us to say to whom the words "Come, O blessed
of my Father, inherit the kingdom prepared for you from
the foundation of the world" (Mt 25:34) are going to be
addressed. That is part of God's freedom.
      Secondly, we must respect man's freedom. In the life of
the men and women about us, who can say with certitude
what it is they perceive? Indeed, can we say of ourselves
what it is that we perceive? The human life of each person
and each community of people is rich in possibilities,

possibilities that cannot be limited by our thoughts and judgements on them. "There are more things in heaven and earth, Horatio, than are dreamt of in your philosophy."[19] The human heart has depths that we cannot plumb. It has values, commitments, choices and activities that cannot be expressed in so many formulae. The innermost depths of man's being cannot be reduced to the exterior manifestations of that being. So, just as the believer cannot be identified by the truths and formulae of the faith that he proclaims, likewise the non-believer cannot be identified with his conscious and free affirmations. The exterior manifestations can be pointers, signs of my belief or of my unbelief, but they do not express the whole mystery of my life and very often the exterior manifestations do not in fact express the deepest aspects of our life commitments, of our relationship with God, of our faith. They do not always accurately express our interiority. We recall the words of St Paul: "I do not understand my own actions. For I do not do what I want, but I do the very thing I hate" (Rom 7:15). And just as we apply this to ourselves, so also we can apply it to the non-believer.

It is interesting that we define our brothers and sisters in negative terms: *non*-believers. This underlines the extent to which we conceive of faith as a thing to be grasped, data to be accepted, rather than a relationship to be entered into. We speak of the "deposit" of faith and almost inevitably tend to imagine it as something into which we can dip in order to increase our faith. Again, it underlines the almost exclusively intellectualist understanding of faith. When, however, faith is stressed as a relationship, such an understanding does not deny the intellectual aspect of it but is does relativize it. The non-believer does not see the centre of his or her life in negative terms. Their "non-belief" is for them peripheral to their existence and probably in the vast majority of cases does not even impinge on their consciousness. It is simply not significant. For that reason, when we view men and women as "non-believers" our view of them is totally arbitrary and does not take them seriously.

In the light of all this, we ask ourselves if we should

speak at all of "believers" and "non-believers". Should we
not rather position ourselves before the profound mystery
of God who has created each and every one and who calls
all to enter into communion with him? If a man or woman
professes his or her disbelief in Jesus Christ, I have no right
to say that such a person does believe but does not really
know it. At the same time, I have no right to claim that
a man's explicit proclamation exhausts the possibilities of
his being. I cannot force anyone to accept my convictions
of conscience or project them on to him in spite of his
explicit protestations. Such would be to disrespect his liberty
and the liberty of God. It would also be to claim that I have
a monopoly of knowledge regarding the Holy Spirit's ways
of incorporating human beings into Christ, of inserting them
in the communion of the Godhead. But when I say that faith
and salvation are in and through Jesus Christ, I cannot deny
my own convictions, my own understanding of the faith,
even though I realize that my "understanding' of the faith
does not exhaust its contents. I am aware that "my
knowledge of faith is nevertheless everywhere followed by
doubt as its shadow."[20] It is not arrogant to suppose that
one's faith is true. If I didn't believe it to be true, it would
be stupid to hold it. We can never have a true relationship
with people of other faiths if we are not, first of all, true
to our own.

God wishes all people to be saved and this salvation is
effected through Jesus Christ in the Holy Spirit. Since God
is free and can do what he wishes, we do not have to worry
as if the salvation of our brothers and sisters depended
entirely on us. This is not to misunderstand the nature of
the Church nor the centrality of her mission to evangelize.
The Church is not, in the first place, called to pass on certain formulae regarding God and his plan of salvation. The
Church's primary duty is to collaborate with Jesus Christ
in being the "light of the world", the "salt of the earth",
the "leaven in the mass". What we as Church are called
to be in the world is precisely to be Christ rather than to
proclaim creeds. The proclamation of a creed is only meaningful when it helps to explain a life. It is the life that is

lived in Christ that is vital for the Church and the world. We will return to this point more at length when we come to discuss the Church and her Mission.

When we realize that the fount of our faith is nothing less than God himself, then we become aware that the consequence of this faith is to insert us into love, opening us up vertically to God himself who is love and horizontally to all our brothers and sisters. For that reason faith is the breaking down of barriers, the widening of horizons. Christian faith is *universal* in the deepest sense of the terms. It is for *all* and affects the *whole* man. It is not a particular ideology, not the foundation of a specific cult. It is not for a determined race or people. Faith puts me into a relationship not only with God but with all humanity, in fact, with the whole universe, and the deeper my own faith, the deeper will be my relationships with God, with my brothers and sisters and with the created world about me. When we find ourselves putting up barriers to people, to their culture and traditions, then we realize that we are not living out of our Christian faith.

A false security of faith

A narrow concept of faith can even be an obstacle for us, for it can lead to a certain centering of ourselves, seeing *our* conscious convictions as the centre from which to judge others, seeking in them the reflection of our own faith. True faith, however, opens us to the complexities of humanity, to its searching for meaning, to its questions which so often are disturbing and discomfiting. This opening of ourselves to others leads to a deepening of faith, for it leads us to the God who works in diverse ways, to an ever richer appreciation of his plan of salvation for all mankind. We thereby avoid the ever-present temptation to reduce God's plan to our own convictions, to our own little way of seeing things. Our faith is precisely what enables us to abandon our little securities in order to give ourselves in trust to the God who has called us, to leave behind "our country and our kindred and our father's house to the land that he will show us'' (cf. Gen 12:1). The certitude of faith is what enables us to enter the insecurity of a road on which we choose to remain before the unknown of the divine activity in the world. The security of faith stems from the conviction that the world is the result of God's love, and that this love constitutes the very pole of humanity. Entering into contact with our non-Christian brothers and sisters means entering upon that road, abandoning the false security of our own convictions, in order to discover that God is indeed God, infinitely greater that we can think or imagine.

We can say that faith is present from that moment in which man turns to God in order to seek the fulfilment of his life. And normally this turning to God to seek the fulfilment of one's life takes place within the context of a religion, within the religion into which one is born or in which one finds a response to one's search for meaning. The religions are the normal way in which man turns to God.

> If on principle a non-Christian religion could not and ought not to have absolutely any positive influence on the supernatural salvation of a man who is not a Christian, then the salvation of such a man would be conceived as totally non-social and non-historical − and this contradicts the historical and social (ecclesial) character of Christianity itself.[21]

For that reason it would seem incontrovertible that saving faith is to be found within one's religion, especially where the religion in question has for hundreds, if not for thousands, of years nourished the spiritual lives of millions of people. The response that we give to God is not given from some ahistorical stance but from the existential situation of time and place in which we find ourselves and this means from the religious environment in which we live. Christian faith stands in a special relationship with the Christian religion which has as its centre the Incarnation, life, death and resurrection of Jesus Christ. Our faith is constantly oriented to these events, from which faith is fed and which are in their turn nourished by faith. It is faith that enables man to appropriate these events, this Event, to himself so that he is enabled to identify with this supreme response to God's love. And yet once more we must insist in the double aspect — faith as grace and faith as a human decision. Faith is obedience to the will of God, submission to him, and yet, paradoxically, it is freedom, for through it we are empowered to be truly human, free from the apparent meaninglessness of human existence, from the constant threat of death in all its forms. Obedience to God is the road to true freedom. For that reason true faith is that which enables man to be the fully realized man of which St Irenaeus speaks,[22] to live in the resurrection. In the measure in which a specific religion enables its adherents to discover this dying/rising process at the heart of human existence, in that measure the religion is a vehicle of faith, in that measure we can see it as Christian.

Religions can be viewed in many different ways but all of them are in some way regarded as ways in which to discover something of God (or of Being if one prefers), a discovery that is perceived as salvific for one's life and is appropriated as such in faith. I recognize that the truth of this statement is open to debate and can be substantiated only by an *a posteriori* examination of each specific religion. But even a superficial examination of the great religions of the world would have to admit that in them are to be found elements of what we regard as true revelation, elements which contribute to placing man in a situation where a true genuine relationship with the one God could take place. This implies that in each of the world religions there is to be found genuine grace. This is not to make Christians out of all religious people or Christian Church out of all religions. To be a Christian in the formal sense requires the gift of Baptism, the formal sacramental incorporation into Christ, and it is the community of such believers that constitute the Church. But it does mean that salvation is to be found in the other religions and that it is mediated through these other religions.

NOTES

1. Cf. Karl Rahner, "Christianity's Absolute Claim", *Theological Investigations* Vol XXI (Darton, Longman and Todd, London 1988), pp. 171–184.

2. On this topic, of interest are: Walter Kasper, *An Introduction to Christian Faith* (Paulist Press, New York 1980); Joseph Ratzinger, *Introduction to Christianity* (Search Press, London 1969); Jean Mouroux, *I Believe. The Personal Structure of Faith* (Chapman, London 1959); Karl Rahner, *Foundations of Christian Faith* (Darton, Longman and Todd, London 1978); Hans Küng, *On Being a Christian* (Collins, London 1977); Gerald O'Collins, *Fundamental Theology* (Darton, Longman and Todd, London 1981); the article "Faith" in *Sacramentum Mundi* Vol. II (Burns and Oates, London and Herder and Herder, New York 1968), pp. 310–326.

3. Hans Küng, *On Being a Christian*, p. 161.

4. Wolfhart Pannenberg, "Anthropology and the Question of God", in *Basic Questions in Theology* Vol III (SCM Press, London 1973), p. 82.

5. S.Th. I, 9. 13, a. 12c.

6. Cf. chapters III and IV of the *Dogmatic Constitution of the Catholic Faith* of Vatican I, D. 3008–3020.

7. We will not elaborate here on the centrality of the Resurrection for Christian faith. Pannenberg states it well when he writes: "The resurrection of Jesus is the event which was, historically speaking, the point of departure for the history of Christendom. In particular, the Easter event forms the starting point for the history of faith in Christ. And this starting point is at the same time the permanent, substantial foundation for that faith. Historical origin and substantial foundation are here one . . . The doctrine of the Incarnation only develops in retrospect what the raising of Jesus means for the whole of his earthly activity and his person. And finally it is only in the light of the raising of Jesus that his death takes on the meaning of the vicariously accomplished reconciliation of mankind" (Wolfhart Pannenberg, *The Apostles' Creed in the Light of Today's Questions* (SCM, London 1972), p. 96.

8. Edward Schillebeeckx, *Theologisch Geloofsverstaan anno 1983*, quoted in Robert J. Schreiter (ed.), *The Schillebeeckx Reader* T. & T. Clark, Edinburgh 1986), p. 114.

9. Dietrich Bonhoeffer, *Letters and Papers from Prison* (SCM Press, London 1971).

10. Juan Alfaro, article on "Faith" in *The Concise Sacramentum Mundi* (Seabury Press, New York 1975), p. 500.

11. The centrality of Christ and of the Incarnation in Christian faith entered the arena of public debate in England with the book *The Myth of God Incarnate*, edited by John Hick (SCM Press, London 1977). Many of the authors in this collection of essays ask the question whether there could be a Christianity without Incarnation, and some would appear to believe that it is possible. See also: *Incarnation and Myth: The Debate Continued* (SCM, London 1979). Also in this connection is Brian Hebblethwaite,

The Incarnation. Collected Essays in Christology (Cambridge University Press, Cambridge 1987).
    12. Cf. E. Schillebeeckx, *Christ the Sacrament of the Encounter with God* (Sheed & Ward, London 1983), especially chapters 1 and 2.
    13. On this point Dermont Lane writes: "When we relocate the mystery of the Incarnation therefore within the context of God's presence throughout creation it becomes clear that the mystery of the Word Incarnate is not some unnatural or atypical divine gesture. On the contrary the incarnation of God in Jesus is the unambiguous and definitive revelation of a divine presence which is all around us. The Incarnation therefore is not the manifestation of a presence which was previously absent but rather the special incidence of a divine omnipresence in the world at large. Within this unique instance God is at his most typical in that the universal self-communication of God throughout the world becomes particularised and personified in Jesus Christ. As such this particularisation and personification of God's self-communication in Jesus is perfectly consistent and quite in character with his overall self-communication in creation." (*The Reality of Jesus*, Veritas, Dublin and Sheed & Ward, London 1975), p. 136.
    14. Cf. Karl Rahner, *Foundations of Christian Faith*, pp. 140ff.
    15. Karl Rahner, "Christ in the Non-Christian Religions", in George Gispert-Sauch (ed.), *God's Word Among Men* (Vidyajyoti, Delhi 1973), p. 97; see also: Karl Rahner, *Foundations of Christian Faith,* pp. 315–321.
    16. Karl Rahner, "The Act of Faith and the Content of Faith", *Theological Investigations* Vol. XXI (Darton, Longman and Todd, London 1988), pp. 151–161. The original essay appeared in 1982.
    17. *Ibid.,* pp. 153–4.
    18. *Ibid.,* p. 158.
    19. *Hamlet* I, v. 166.
    20. Hans Küng, *On Being a Christian*, p. 163.
    21. Karl Rahner, "Christ in the Non-Christian Religions", p. 97.
    22. "God's glory is man alive; and man's life consists in beholding God." This most famous sentence of Irenaeus beautifully expresses the dignity of man and his total dependence on God (*Adv. Haer.* IV, 20, 7).

5

The Church

Of all branches of theology, ecclesiology is perhaps the one that has been most affected by the deliberations of the Second Vatican Council. Indeed, the central question of that Council was none other than: "Church, what do you say of yourself?" Pope Paul VI, in his address to the Council Fathers at the opening of the Second Session, said:

> The time has now come, we believe, when the truth regarding the Church of Christ should be examined, coordinated and expressed. . . For this reason, the principal concern of this session of the Council will be to examine the intimate nature of the Church and to express in human language, so far as that is possible, a definition which will best reveal the Church's real, fundamental constitution and manifest its manifold mission of salvation.[1]

The most influential document emanating from the Council was its Dogmatic Constitution on the Church, *Lumen Gentium*. This document constitutes, as it were, the hinge upon which all the deliberations of the Council turned. In the opening paragraph of Chapter One of *Lumen Gentium*, dedicated significantly to the "Mystery of the Church", we find the Church described as follows:

> By her relationship with Christ, the Church is a kind of sacrament, or sign of intimate union with God and of the unity of all mankind. She is also an instrument for the achievement of such union and unity.

Edward Schillebeeckx called this text, "one of the most fortunate passages" in the Constitution, and said, "I personally think that this confession of faith is one of the most charismatically inspired texts of the Council."[2] Later, in Paragraph 48, the Church is described as "the universal sacrament of salvation". What is meant by calling the Church a "sacrament"? Let us quote from Schillebeeckx again:

> The Church is the realising sign – the sacrament – of the mutual unity or *communio* of the whole of mankind, in and through her union with the living God. She is the community among men by virtue of their communion with God, the life or the living one. In this universal communion, the Church fulfils a sacramental task, that is to say, she is the effective sign of this communion. She is the effective sign not on her own account but because of the unity, peace and justice of God among men – the Church is only an 'instrument' of God's unifying acts of salvation in this world and thus bound to service. At the same time, she is also the *sign*, because this mediatory realisation by the Church is accomplished in a sign, that is to say, the Church is the momentous visible form or meaningful presence in this world of an already accomplished communion of men – or a communion that accomplishes itself in *metanoia* in and through their explicit community with God in Christ.[3]

When we say that the Church is the "universal sacrament of salvation" we are immediately underlining what is her function in the world. She must be the visible sign and instrument of the salvation in the world.

> As a sacrament, the Church has the task of making historically visible and present what is already implicitly active in the whole community of men, but is still looking for an explicit, concrete form. In other words, the Church is the realisation of community among men, because she is herself *community* – the people of God and therefore the community of brothers. It is in this way that she is the 'sign set up among the people'.[4]

The sacramentality of the Church is closely bound up with the concept of "mystery". The two words – sacrament and mystery – are intimately related, for the Latin word *"sacramentum"* was the normal translation of the Greek word *"mysterion"*.[5] Very often in St Paul and the Fathers the word "mystery" refers to God's plan of salvation, especially as it was in the mind of God, especially the Christ event. Gradually the word "sacrament" became more identified with the plan of God as it found and finds expression in this world. For this reason to call the Church a sacrament emphasizes two aspects: one, that which is visible, that she is a sign signifying something; and two, that which is invisible, her mystical element, that which is signified. We must never forget either of the two, as both are necessary for a true grasp of the nature of the Church, and the visible aspect can only be understood in the light of the invisible or mystical aspect. The "mystery" of the Church is always the mystery of God himself, offered to man in the Church, under the veil of her humanness. This mystery of God appears most concretely and fully in the mystery of Christ in whose person true human nature and true divine nature are found "without confusion". In him God is present as a man among men. This, of course, does not mean that those who saw the man Jesus, who lived with him, touched him, saw God directly, immediately. For many of them, they saw only a simple Galilean. Yet others experienced in Jesus the nearness of the divinity. Through him they were enabled to enter into the presence of God. His humanity was both the veil of his divinity and its mediator. That is why we call Jesus the "sacrament" of God, for in him we find a *sign* of God, of his presence, his inner life, his will for us and for the world, a sign of God's self-communication to the world. But Jesus was not just a sign of God, he was an *effective sign*, a sign which makes present that which it signifies, an *instrument* which makes present the reality of God. Christ is the sacrament — the sign and instrument — of God's encounter with man and of man's encounter with God or, to put it in another way, Christ is the sacrament — the sign and instrument — of salvation.

The mystery of the Church is the continuation of the mystery of Christ.

If Christ is the sacrament of God, the Church is for us the sacrament of Christ; she represents him, in the full and ancient meaning of the term, she really makes him present. She not only carries on his work but she is his very continuation, in a sense far more real than that in which it can be said that any human institution is its founder's continuation.[6]

And, just as the people of Israel needed to have their eyes opened by the gracious gift of faith in order to recognize God present in the carpenter from Nazareth so likewise we need to have our eyes opened by the same gift of faith in order to see the Mystery and enter into it. The Mystery of Christ continues in the Mystery of the Church. What is primordial and fundamental in the Church is therefore her relationship with Christ. Christ is, in history, the triumphal presence of the mercy of God, of his love. In him God has embraced the world. In the Incarnation God took to himself the whole of humanity, in its sinful, fallen condition, and in so doing he redeemed it, saved it. Redemption or salvation can be seen as God taking a fallen world to himself. In Jesus Christ, God's final word on the destiny of mankind has been spoken and that word is a word of love, of forgiveness, of reconciliation. In Jesus Christ, God's grace is permanently in the world, not now as an abstract, invisible reality but as something concrete, historical. In this portion of the world, the humanity of Jesus Christ, the salvation of the whole is sacramentally present. In him, humanity in its entirety, humanity as a whole unit, has been saved. And this sacrament of salvation is continued in and through the Church.

While it must be admitted that the terminology of "sacrament" applied to the Church is of relatively recent origin, the reality is as ancient as the Church herself, and the Council Fathers saw the term as most apt to express the deeper aspects of the Church's nature, especially her mission to the world. For too long, the nature of the Church had been somewhat inward looking, thinking primarily in terms of her visible structures, her hierarchy, law, cult, etc. but all of these are means to help express her inner core and do not form the inner core itself. By emphasizing the Church as a sacrament, the fact is at once underlined that the Church points to something beyond herself, beyond her visible structures; a sign is a true sign in the measure in which

it points beyond itself to what it is supposed to signify.
Now the Church is called to be a sign of the "intimate union
with God and the unity of all mankind"; or, in other words,
she is called to be a "sign of salvation". Christ was sent
by the Father to be the sign and instrument of salvation
for the whole world and he in his turn chose to continue
this mission in and through the Church: "*As* the Father has
sent me, *even so* I send you" (Jn 20:21). The Church, upon
which is poured out the Spirit of Jesus, is now the sacrament of salvation in the world. And this means that the
Church is the sacrament of salvation for non-believers as
for believers, for as Karl Rahner has pointed out:

> . . . God's grace actually effects the salvation of humankind
> far beyond the radius of Catholics and of baptized Christians
> and does this for the most part without the saved being incor-
> porated into the visible Church by Baptism; and when a
> Catholic Christian at the same time believes that the salvation
> of these innumerable people has, nevertheless, a relationship
> to the Church, then this statement about the Church as univer-
> sal sacrament of the salvation of all mankind takes on
> tangible meaning.[7]

It must be clearly understood that what makes the Church
to be the sign and instrument of salvation is precisely her
profound and intimate relation with Christ. She is the Body
of Christ.

The Church as necessary for salvation

Seeing the Church primarily in terms of "sacrament" (but
ever conscious of the invisible as well as the visible aspects)
shifts the centre of interest from herself to her mission in
the world. For so long the Church was seen primarily in
terms of the "sanctuary of salvation", the "ark" into which
all those who were to be saved had to be gathered – and
if they were not, then they were irretrievably lost! As Vatican
I put it, "Who is not in this ark will perish in the flood."[8]
It was this mental image which gave an interpretation to
the phrase of Cyprian, "no salvation outside the Church",
that now seems unbelievable. The claim that the Church

is necessary for salvation arises from her relationship with Christ, the mediator of salvation for the whole world. If she were not united with Christ, if she did not have within her the Spirit of Christ, then it would be both preposterous and outrageously arrogant for the Church to make such a claim. Her claim can be understood and appreciated only from within the position of belief, of faith in Christ.

> The idea of sacramentality evokes the indissoluble union, in the Spirit, between Christ and his Church. We cannot know the Church, believe in her, love her, live her life, without finding therein the very actuality of Christ.[9]

Likewise faith in the Church leads us to Christ present in her as her heart. Without faith, the Church is another grouping of people, organized, structured in a particular manner but nonetheless a merely human phenomenon. But for those with faith the Church is in a very special and real way the Body of Christ. William of Saint-Thierry, writing on the Sacrament of the Altar, refers to the "threefold Body of the Lord":

> Whenever the intelligent reader finds in a book anything about the flesh or body of the divine Jesus, he may apply this threefold definition of his flesh or body. . . For he must think in one way of that flesh or body which hung on the Cross and is sacrificed on the altar, in another way of his flesh or body which is abiding life to the person who receives it in Communion, and in yet another way of that flesh and body which is the Church. . . Not that we would depict Christ as having three bodies, like Geryon in the fable, since the Apostle testifies that the body of Christ is one. But the mind or heart makes the distinction with a certain relation to faith, though the reality maintains the undefiled truth in its simplicity. For this threefold nature of the body of the Lord is to be understood exactly as the body of the Lord himself is understood, according to its essence, its unity and its effect. For the body of Christ, exactly as it is in itself, is offered to all as the food of eternal life and unites in its life those who receive it faithfully both by the love of the Spirit and by a sharing in its own nature, the living head of the body of the Church.[10]

Thus, the essential structure of the Church underlines in a powerful way the raison d'être of her existence. She is to witness to the presence of the Lord, for only in this way can she be a sign of salvation for the whole of humanity and only in this way can she be an instrument of salvation for the same humanity. Furthermore, she will be an instrument of salvation in the measure in which she is a sign of salvation. And because salvation consists in the "intimate union with God and the union of all mankind", the only way she can be a sign of this salvation is through the life of charity: "By this all men will know that you are my disciples, if you have love for one another" (Jn 13:35). Charity is the soul of the Church, and because of God's self-revelation, it could not be otherwise. In other words, the Church is called to be the sacrament of the love of God in the world and for the world. The Church is not a power within the world, concerned with the defence of her own structures as power structures. Rather, all the structures of the Church must be continually examined so that they are truly at the service of her sacramentality, really enabling her to be ever more fully a sign and instrument of salvation.

Thus the visible, historical community of believers in Jesus Christ is part of that process of salvation which began with creation and which will come to its completion only with the Second Coming of Christ. It is therefore united with every moment of the process although it is more clearly understood in terms of the Incarnation rather than the creation. There is, however, a sense in which the Church as a community of faith has existed from the beginning, understanding faith, as we have said, as the response to God who invites us to share in his life, as the way in which man enters into that relationship for which we were created in the first place. There have always been people who have made that response and, as such, there have always been men and women of faith. In each person who enters into this world the loving mystery of creation takes place. God calls each one by name and no one is excluded by God from this covenant, this election, this grace. And just as the event of Jesus Christ is a "light for revelation to the Gentiles" (Lk 2:32) and in him "all flesh shall see the salvation of God" (Lk 3:6) so likewise the Church, for this same Jesus now lives in his Church, his Body. For that reason, the principle "no salvation outside the Church" "does not propose to concentrate on the boundaries of the Church but, rather, on the contrary, it seeks to highlight the universal mediatory role of Christ's Church."[11] Karl Rahner, commenting on the Church as the universal sign of salvation wrote:

> The Church viewed as tangible, historical, and institutional entity is the abiding presence of Christ in history. This Jesus Christ is the historically concrete presence of God's promise to all mankind at all times and in all places, and the Church is the reality of God's historical promise to himself to all humankind, the reality which always continues to make this self-promise historically present and which constantly bears witness to its irrevocability, and it does this for all people whether they have lived before or after Christ and not only when these people have become members of the visible Church by baptism, something that for the most part does not actually happen. The Church is the promise of salvation precisely for those as well who are not part of its visible membership. The incorporation of a person by Baptism into the visible Church is first of all the continuation of this sign of salvation in time and in history for the people who are not members of the Church in a visible way."[12]

Christ alone is the perfected sacrament. "In him alone shines forth all the love of the Father and the power of the Holy Spirit. All other signs of God's love and presence are valid signs, visible and effective for the salvation of the world, only in view of him and in him."[13] This brings us to the Trinitarian dimension of the Church.

The Trinitarian dimension of the Church

The Eastern tradition likes to call the Church the "Icon of the Trinity" thereby stressing the understanding of the Church as communion, relationships. The world exists because God our Father wished to share his life, his happiness with other, created beings. It stems from the innermost nature of God as love, as self-communication. His plan is that all mankind achieve their final destiny, eternal life, union with him. He wishes that this union with him be truly loving, truly personal, and so he granted to man freedom, the capacity to choose him. But man abused this freedom, rejecting the invitation. Nevertheless, in spite of mankind's rejection of his plan, God did not repent or change his plan but rather brings it about in Christ. Because of man's rejection, God does not cease to be a God of love, does not cease to be Father. And so Christ, the Only Begotten Son, the eternally perfect response to the Father's love, becomes man and in him humanity is able to give a perfect response to God. Thus Christ becomes the universal means of salvation for fallen man. In Christ humanity in the depths of its existence responds to God. In and through Jesus Christ God is committed to bringing about the salvation of each and every human being, fulfilling their deepest aspirations. He does so without doing violence to man's nature, without destroying the way in which he created man. Through Christ, mankind, in its full humanity, is enabled to respond to God. Salvation is incarnational, and God has chosen to continue this incarnational aspect of the saving process in and through the Church.

And so we have the Church, which continues to make sacramentally present the salvation that is Jesus Christ. Christ is the head of the Church in every sense. As such he is the means by which the world becomes the world of the Father, becomes a filial world, and we must always remember that Father and Son are relational terms. In the humanity of Christ creation achieves its fullness, and in the Church, this process of drawing all earth, all creation, to its fullness continues. In the risen Christ it has already taken place − but it awaits the insertion of each individual into that fullness. For that reason the full realization of the process will take place only in the *Parousia*. Because of its relationship with Christ, the Church possesses the fullness already, in germ, as it were, and this is manifested in the Eucharist, in Holy Communion. This is possible because the Father and the Son have poured out on the Church the principle of their union, the Holy Spirit, who, as we have mentioned already, is, as it were, the "bond" between them; and by this pouring out, the Church, the community of believers in Jesus Christ, is thereby capacitated to enter into the same life, the same union. The Spirit is, so to speak, the dynamism of the communion, the vital energy, the one who establishes God's paternity vis-à-vis us, and our filiation vis-à-vis him. Through the Holy Spirit, we become one with Christ, one Body with him, sharing in one faith, the one response to God, enter into the one relationship. The Spirit is he who unifies our diversity without destroying it, gathers together the different gifts he himself has distributed throughout the members of the Church so that they form one united witness to God's love. It is in the Spirit that we are re-created, born again; it is the Spirit who effects our death to sin and our resurrection to the new life of grace.

Thus, the Trinitarian dimension of the Church is at its very heart and, once again, this is so because of her relationship with Christ. This point keeps coming up over and over again. But to say that the Trinity is operative in the Church is not to say that it is only operative in the visible, organized society that is historically manifested. The sign is not identical with the reality signified – it points to it in a true, authentic way, but the reality surpasses the sign and in this case infinitely so. Yet, God has willed to unite the sign inseparably to the reality. We might compare it to the sign and the reality of the Eucharist. The bread and wine, "fruit of the earth and work of human hands", are signs which signify the reality of our communion with Christ but the reality of that communion is infinitely greater than the sign. Yet, if the signs are not there then the reality is not present; if the visible, material elements of bread and wine are not available then the Eucharist cannot be celebrated. Again, we are reminded that the Church is composed of two aspects: the mystical and the material, and the two must be kept in tension. The temptation is to exaggerate the one at the expense of the other but to do so is to be unjust to both, to disrespect God's freedom in the offer of his plan of salvation and man's freedom in responding to that plan.

It brings us to the first point of this chapter, namely, that we are dealing with the *mystery* of the Church, a mystery which is none other than the Mystery of God himself. This is not to opt out of striving for understanding but a gentle reminder that what we are seeking is precisely the understanding of the Word of God which by definition can never simply be a word of man. God's Word infinitely surpasses man's word.

The "marks" of the Church

Naturally, as an historical reality, the Church is in a state of constant change. Each new age, each new situation calls forth a new form of her existence. Yet there must be something that perdures and this perduring element we may call her essence. This essence must be distinguishable in the community of believers — although not necessarily in the individual believer. The Church is first and foremost an assembly, an *ekklesia*, a *convocatio*, a calling together, a community of believers, and it is to the community we look in order to find how we can distinguish the perduring essence of the Church. Traditionally, we have been given four characteristics that distinguish the Church as founded by Jesus Christ: she is one, holy, catholic and apostolic. Even though these four characteristics or "marks" have been described as insufficient in themselves, yet, understood correctly, they do enable us to distinguish the Church of Christ from any possible pretender to that title. In the measure in which the Church is really, existentially one, holy, catholic and apostolic — in that measure it is true.

The Church is one. Obviously, "one" here cannot refer to one visible group of Christians to the exclusion of other groups of Christians. "One", as a mark of the Church, refers rather to that unity which is found in the Church. The Church and unity are inseparably joined because they have one and the same foundation: love. When one looks around the Christian world one cannot but be struck by the divisions, oftentimes profound, to be found among the different groups calling themselves the Christian Church. One of the saddest aspects of a visit to the Holy Land is precisely the experience of this division which becomes so evident there. There is no doubt that this division is a scandal, a stumbling block for those called to faith, a stumbling block also for those striving to grow in the faith they have embraced. For the Church must be one because she is one in her origin, one in her message, one in her faith, one in the Spirit which animates her. The communion effected by Jesus Christ cannot be many. Such would be a contradiction in terms. The Church must be the one People of God, the one Body of Christ, the one Temple of the Holy Spirit. The New Testament is unequivocal about this:

> I therefore, a prisoner for the Lord, beg you to lead a life worthy of the calling to which you have been called, with all lowliness and meekness, with patience, forbearing one another in love, eager to maintain the unity of the Spirit in the bond of peace. There is one body and one Spirit, just as you are called to the one hope that belongs to your call, one Lord, one faith, one Baptism, one God and Father of us all, who is above all and through all and in all. (Eph 4:1–6)

However, the one Church is present in distinct and different Churches – the Church in Rome, the Church in Jerusalem, the Church in Dublin, the Church in Jos, etc. Thus, we have local Churches, regional Churches, just as there were in apostolic times. The one Church of the New Testament is composed of many different Churches, arising from the plurality of cultures and peoples in which the Church has taken root as also arising from the plurality of gifts which God has chosen to bestow on each one. Likewise in the New Testament, we find plurality of forms of worship, of ecclesiastical organization, of theologies – but all these pluralities do not destroy the unity. What is important is that each one has the same God, the same Lord, the same Spirit, the same faith and hope, bound together by the same love. Differences in themselves do not divide. On the contrary, they can be extraordinarily enriching, provided that they are not exclusive differences, that they do not deliberately exclude other forms of being Church, for then they would impoverish the unity of the Church, diminish it, and so in the process diminish her credibility, her witness and her service in the world.

Here we cannot go into the whole question of ecumenism. Suffice it to say that the unity of the Church is something that springs from *within*, not imposed from *without*; it is a unity which not only does not exclude diversity but positively demands it − if it is to be true to the triune God and to the nature of man in the world. Of course, the unity of the Church is a unity that constantly seeks expression in the world − through shared prayer, shared profession of faith, shared celebration − but not one that demands uniformity in prayer, in our profession of faith, nor uniform modes of celebrating it. Because of our condition as human beings, subject to the onward march of time, we must be continually seeking this unity of the Church, this unity of faith, hope and love. There will be times when we achieve this better than at other times, there will be places where it is clearer than elsewhere. So there will be, from a human point of view, greater or lesser expressions of the fundamental unity of the Church − and this underlines the constant need for purification, the constant need for the response to the call: "Repent, and believe in the gospel" (Mk 1:15). This call is addressed as much to the members of the Church as to those outside. Evangelization is a process applicable to the Church herself as well as to her ministry to the world. Indeed, in the measure in which she is herself evangelized will she evangelize − and vice versa!

The Church is holy. Holiness is the ambient in which God lives. God is holy and everything else is holy only in the measure in which it is identified or related with him. Jesus is "the holy one of God" precisely because in him God is present and through him we are enabled to enter into a relationship with God. Through our faith in him we become holy. The holiness of the Church is therefore directly dependent on its relationship with Christ, a relationship that is initiated in Baptism and that will come to its fullness in the *Parousia*. For this reason, the holiness of the Church is the affirmation of her identity with Christ, an identity that will never be broken. The holiness of the Church underlines what the Church, understood as a community of believers, is called to be. Once again it manifests the tension between the "already" and the "not yet", the fact that we are sinners and yet that we have been made "sons in the Son".

Likewise, it is this relationship with Christ that underpins the sanctifying activity of the Church. The Spirit, by virtue of whom we are enabled to be the instruments of salvation, works through us despite our inadequacy. The work of sanctification is effective, even though subjectively it may not be realized in its fullness, due to the defectibility of the instruments. Thus, between the Church as members of the Body of Christ and the Spirit which vivifies that Body there is a tension, a tension which constantly calls the Church to total fidelity to the Spirit who is at work in her. Once again we see that from man's point of view the sanctity of the Church is a task upon which we must constantly work, while from God's point of view the sanctity of the Church is ever perfect because it is none other than the sanctity of God himself. Thus the whole life of the Church is an unremitting striving for the fidelity to the Spirit whose temple she is, a constant fidelity to the head whose Body she is, a constant fidelity to the husband whose Spouse she is.

And this striving is precisely the acceptance of the paschal event in which she is born, this insertion into the death and resurrection of Christ, from which event she was generated, lives and comes to her fulfilment. She must die to the flesh in order to be born in the Spirit. Because materially she is made up of human beings, the Church is a Church of sinners, but because she is born in the Spirit, she is holy, and it is this latter point that is primary.

As real as sin may be, it does not define the essence of the Church but rather her "mal-essence", which is rather ours than hers. The Church is not a land of choice for sin but rather a territory unjustly overtaken.

In order to understand the Church in its pristine essence one must return to the notion of holiness. No human analogy can express the paradox of a community which human misery can disfigure but cannot determine. The Church exists as an apostolic community of the faithful gathered together by faith in the resurrection, only because a love stronger than death and betrayal supports her. The holiness of the Church is the holiness of Christ, and man's sin in the Church cannot be placed on the same level as the holiness of Christ's presence. Sin comes from man. It cannot prevail against Christ and banish him from his own house. Holiness outlives sin and in the final analysis denies it. Sin is in the Church as that which wounds her, never as that which constitutes her.[14]

As the Body of Christ, the Church is in communion with grace, communion with the life of God. But because this Body of Christ is made up of members who are still on the pilgrim road, materially the Church will not be completely holy until the end. From this point of view the holiness of the Church is eschatologically conditioned.

The Church is catholic. The proper name of the Church is "catholic", universal. This is not because the Church is spread throughout the world or because it can count its numbers in hundreds of millions. The Church was as truly catholic on Pentecost Sunday when its members numbered but a handful, as it is today. Catholicity is not a question of geography or numbers; it is something intrinsic to her nature, something that is found in the deepest aspect of her being, for the catholicity of the Church springs from her centre, from Christ himself, true God and true man. In Christ, the Church embraces all men and the whole man. In the Church, Christ gathers all into one single body. This is the catholicity expressed by St Augustine when he writes:

You unite together the inhabitants of the cities, the different peoples, nay, the whole human race, by belief in our common origin, so that men are not satisfied in being joined together, but become in some sort, brothers.[15]

Ignatius of Antioch, writing in the early years of the second century, was the first to use the word "catholic" for the Church: "Where the bishop is, there is the community, just as where Jesus is, there is the catholic Church."[16]

Thus the word "catholic", as applied to the Church, carries two connotations. First, it implies the idea of authenticity. The catholic Church is the true, authentic Church. Secondly, it implies the idea of the Church in its totality, its universality. The catholic Church is the whole Church, the universal Church.

The Church was born in an ambient of true catholicity as is clear from the Book of Acts:

> Now there were dwelling in Jerusalem Jews, devout men from every nation under heaven. And at his sound the multitude came together, and they were bewildered, because each one heard them speaking in his own language. And they were amazed and wondered, saying, "Are not all these who are speaking Galileans? And how is it that we hear, each of us, in his own native language? Parthians and Medes and Elamites and residents of Mesopotamia, Judaea and Cappadocia, Pontus and Asia, Phrygia and Pamphylia, Egypt and the parts of Libya belonging to Cyrene, and visitors from Rome, both Jews and proselytes, Cretans and Arabians, we hear them telling in our own tongues the mighty works of God." (Acts 2:5–11)

On this point Elias Zoghby has written:

> It is in this climate of universality that God has willed that the Church be born and it is in this same climate that he wills that she should live. She must receive all peoples equally. She must propose to them in their own language and according to their own genius the same faith and the same baptism. The Church must allow no obstacle to come between her and her obligation to go out to all peoples, and plant herself in the whole of the inhabited world − neither obstacles of language, nor of colour nor of race. "Now the company of those who believed", says the Author of Acts who has just enumerated their diverse origins, "were of one heart and soul" (Acts 4:32). The day when the Church avoids such a climate and seeks instead to become the fief of a "chosen people" or of a particular country, on that day she renounces in fact her catholicity and simply becomes a particular or local church for she has then

substituted the unity of Pentecost for the uniformity of human endeavour.[17]

In order to be truly catholic, the Church must constantly strive to become incarnate in each community of peoples. The encounter between the Church and the various cultures is one of profound mutual interaction.

> To be truly universal, the Church must not only make the people hers, but she herself must become them.[18]

This is more pressing than ever before. For the first time in her history the Church in this century has become indeed a world Church, present, even if only in a small way, in almost every culture and peoples, and all of those local Churches must have equal rights within the one Church. Brotherhood must not only be preached, it must also be lived. The Catholic Church, because of its enormous numbers must ever strive to avoid the temptation to constitute itself a Latin Church, imposing a Latin culture on the peoples to whom she has proclaimed and is proclaiming the Good News of Jesus Christ. There must be unity but a unity that is truly catholic. The young Churches of Africa must be allowed to become truly the catholic Church in Africa and not just the Latin Church in Africa. In this the role of the individual bishops and especially the role of the Episcopal Conferences is of vital importance. The Church must be aware of the threats of juridicism, paternalism and particularism to her catholicism and fight against them.

There is a sense in which the Church is a "particular" Church, always has been and always will, because it is a Church that must of necessity be incarnate in history. As with Christ, the Church takes on the particularity, the limitations, imposed by the law of the Incarnation. But it is precisely in this incarnational aspect that she assumes her full universality, her full catholicity. Christ voluntarily took upon himself the limitation of belonging to a particular family, a particular tribe, a particular nation, at a particular time in history. And these same limitations apply to the Church in her incarnational aspect. But just as Christ is "the saviour of all men" (1 Tim 4:10) so also the Church.

This has important repercussions. The catholic Church cannot simply be identified with any one historical manifestation of that Church. It is much wider and deeper than that. To absolutize one historical manifestation of the Church is to destroy its catholicity. It would be to limit, put boundaries on, the Spirit which animates it. An ever fuller catholicity is a task which we must assume continually, a goal to be attained, for it is ever greater than any historical expression of it. In our historical situation catholicity is a goal to be aimed at, a task to be undertaken continually rather than a gift to be enjoyed, a privilege to be savoured. It is because the true Church of Christ must be catholic in the full sense of the term that she can never cease to witness before all men, for only in this way can she discover what it means to be catholic. Catholicity demands mission, and mission must always be catholic if it is to be truly Christian mission.

> The Church will only come to really know herself in the measure in which she becomes truly catholic. . . But can we say that we are really aware of the catholicity of the Church so long as we fail to grasp it in its concreteness, as it actually absorbs values or realities that were, at first, or seemed to be, alien to it?. . . The catholicity of its faith becomes the more manifest when the opportunity offers of being received and thought out afresh by classes and persons hitherto unreached by it. The same applies to the catholicity of all the other well-springs of unity, that is to say, of all the constitutive elements of the Church. In every sphere the Church's potentialities are brought out by being actualized, she is brought to self-understanding by events. That, after all, is the law of all living things.[19]

The day the Church ceases to be missionary, that day she ceases to be Catholic.

> In virtue of this catholicity each part contributes its own gifts to other parts and to the whole Church, so that the whole and each of the parts are strengthened by the common sharing of all things and by the common effort to attain to fullness in unity.[20]

The Church is apostolic. Because of Christ and the pouring out of his Spirit, the Church is one, holy and catholic, but her oneness, holiness and catholicity must be apostolic if they are to be authentic. Hans Küng expresses it well when he writes:

> In our search for unity in diversity, catholicity in identity, holiness in sinfulness, the question of a criterion must always be in our minds. How far can the Church be one, holy and catholic? What is true unity, true catholicity, true holiness? The crucial criterion is expressed in the fourth attribute of the Church: the Church can only be truly one, holy and catholic if it is in all things an *apostolic* Church.[21]

Like the word "catholic", the word "apostolic", as far as can be ascertained, was first used by Ignatius of Antioch[22] and, as we would expect, it underlines the specific relation which the Church has with the apostles. In this way the truth is underlined that the Church must be a *witnessing* Church. Paul gloried in the title "Apostle of Jesus Christ", that is, one who is a witness to the Risen Lord, witness to the resurrection, and one, therefore, called to proclaim that which he has "witnessed".

The concept "apostolic", apart from the idea of one sent to witness, to proclaim a message, also carries the connotation of authority, one sent as a plenipotentiary of Jesus Christ, empowered by Christ to act in his name, and therefore one sent, not by the Church, but by Christ himself. Paul, in writing to the Church in Galatia, presented himself in these words:

> Paul, an apostle – not from men nor through man, but through Jesus Christ and God the Father, who raised him from the dead.(1:1)

Even though a mere, weak, sinful human being, the apostle is nevertheless the instrument of God's grace:

> For I am the least of the apostles, unfit to be called an apostle, because I persecuted the Church of God. But by the grace of God I am what I am, and his grace toward me was not in vain. On the contrary, I worked harder than any of them,

though it was not I, but the grace of God which is with me. Whether then it was I or they, so we preach and so you believed. (1 Cor 15:9–11)

The apostle is one called to preach the Gospel, thereby awakening faith and gathering into one all those who believe. He is to be a minister of the Church, a messenger of God, a witness of the resurrection, an organizer and president of the community of believers. It was as such that the first apostles constituted the foundations upon which the Church was built – but the cornerstone was and continues to be Jesus Christ, who called them and constituted them as apostles.

Through the New Testament and Tradition the ministry of the apostles continues down through the ages. In the New Testament the original ministry of the apostles is conserved, and so today we are enabled to enter into and participate in the original faith and proclamation of the apostles and also to enter into and share in their original ministry. The apostolicity of the Church underlines the fact that the Church is sent to be the servant of the world by ministering to it in such a way that it discovers its own vocation – unity with God.

> The Church, at once a visible assembly and a spiritual community, goes forward together with humanity and experiences the same earthly lot which the world does. She serves as a leaven and as a kind of soul for human society as it is to be renewed in Christ, and transformed into God's family.[23]

Like catholicity, oneness and holiness, the apostolicity of the Church is an ever present challenge to be conquered anew by each Christian and each generation of Christians and this conquest is achieved not through any power in ourselves but by the power of the Spirit of God working in us. Apostolicity is both a gift and a task; as a gift, we realize that there is no room for arrogance, for any sense of superiority or domination; as a task, we realize that there is no room for complacency but are urged rather to zealous, humble service.

If we advance in the attainment of any of the "marks"

of the Church, we advance in all of them. To grow in holiness, for example, is to grow in oneness, in catholicity and apostolicity. It is to enter ever more deeply into that faith in Jesus Christ witnessed to by the apostles and proclaimed in their lives and in their teaching. And this entering into the depths of the faith is made possible by the ongoing activity of the Holy Spirit whom Our Lord has promised will lead us to the fullness of truth. Thus the "marks" of the Church − its oneness, its holiness, its catholicity and its apostolicity − all protect us from deviations in the faith, in our response to God. At the same time they lead us into an ever deeper awareness of that faith, an ever greater commitment to it and an ever growing sensitivity to the manifestations of that faith that we find in the world about us, even outside the boundaries of the visible society of the Church. The "marks" of the Church maintain the openness of the Church to the world, and prevent her from the ever present temptation to close in on herself, on her own interests. They are, as it were, guardians which prevent the Church from absolutizing what is relative, from constituting herself mistress instead of servant, from making herself the world instead of the leaven in the world, making herself the earth instead of the salt of the earth. The "marks" are not static attributes of the Church but dynamic characteristics that must be continually renewed and continually achieved. Fidelity to the "marks" brings about fidelity to the faith and fidelity to the faith means fidelity to Christ.

Earlier in this chapter we mentioned the phrase of Cyprian, "outside the Church there is no salvation", perhaps now we can return to it. How can this phrase be understood in the light of the official declarations that salvation can in fact be found outside the Church?[24] Would it not be better then to jettison the phrase altogether, and state the contrary: outside the Church there is salvation? This positive statement is obviously true, in the light of the statements of the Magisterium of the Church as solemnly made in the Second Vatican Council. Yet the phrase, "outside the Church there is no salvation", does contain a kernel of truth, for it does underline in a striking way the presence of Christ in the Church, and, apart from him, it is our firm belief that salvation cannot be achieved.

In this connection it may be helpful to lay hold of the distinction made by Barth when referring to Christianity. He said that, fundamentally, Christianity is not a religion, it is a faith: "religion is unbelief . . . the one great concern of godless man."[25] While I find it difficult to accept Barth's distinction in its fullness, it does have the virtue of underscoring the fact that Christianity is more than a religion, more than an amalgam of creed, code and cult, and what the extra dimension is, that which sets it apart, is faith — faith understood not in the sense of a creed but as the response to the invitation of God to enter into a relationship with him. Thus what distinguishes the Christian Church from other religions is not its "creed, code and cult" but rather its faith, so that to say that there is no salvation outside the Church is another way of saying that there is no salvation outside the faith, no salvation outside this response to the call of God to share his life, no salvation outside this communion with him.

The Church is the place in humanity where this communion is consciously lived out, where the revelation and response to the revelation of God's communion takes place in a sacramental way. This does not mean that the same communion is not effected in a real but non-sacramental way outside the Church's visible boundaries. The Church in her external aspects can be a hindrance to leading us to the deeper relationship that is faith. Full knowledge of the Creed and even intellectual acceptance of it as true do not necessarily imply the presence of real faith. "Not everyone who says to me 'Lord, Lord,' shall enter the kingdom of heaven, but he who does the will of my Father who is in heaven" (Mt 7:21). Mere verbiage does not of necessity lead to a true communion of souls, to a true conversation. Faith leads us to an internal encounter with the God who has created us, with the God who has saved us, with the God who is within us, and within all creation. The Church properly understood and lived leads us to that encounter, makes it possible, and enables us to perdure in it throughout our lives. It is for this reason that the highest expression of the life of the Church is the Eucharist. There the Church is most perfectly and completely Church.

But we can use the Church wrongly, and so instead of leading us to an ever deeper encounter with the risen Lord it can even become a stumbling block to it. That is why the Church must be in a state of ceaseless reform.

Every renewal of the Church essentially consists in an increase of fidelity to her own calling. Undoubtedly this explains the dynamism of the movement toward unity. Christ summons the Church, as she goes her pilgrim way, to that continual reformation of which she always has need, insofar as she is an institution of men here on earth.[26]

However, the Spirit present in the Church is constantly at work to purify it through the gifts of prophecy and sanctity. The faith as such, if it is not to disappear altogether, has need of the Church for the simple reason that we are not pure spirits – we need the material in order to be. Take away from the Church her "creed, code and cult" and we are left with nothing. It is for this reason that I would find it hard to go the whole way with Barth. Faith needs to be incarnated in some way if it is to be truly faith for men and women. God has given the Church as the continuing incarnation of that faith provided that we realize that the "creed, code and cult" of the Church are the instruments which enable us to articulate and celebrate the faith that we possess and that we do not see them as ends in themselves. The Church seen as a religion is the means Jesus chose to continue his work on earth, his service of being the sacrament, the sign and instrument, of salvation for the whole world. God wants to save us in an incarnational way, entering into dialogue with man, respecting him/her as a free person and so inviting each person to collaborate with the grace that is offered.

The Church is the place where the work of salvation is consciously being brought about. She is, as it were, the conscience of humanity; and just as in a human being consciousness is an essential part of fullness so likewise with

humanity as a whole. Once again, we are reminded of the
fact that God has willed to save man "not merely as individuals without any mutual bonds, but by making them
into a single people, a people which acknowledges him."[27]
Christianity exists for the whole of humanity, and the
Church — i.e., the visible community of all those who
explicitly believe in Jesus Christ — exists as the servant of
that humanity. The Church herself is not the goal of
mankind but God's chosen instrument for the achieving of
that goal. Because the Church is the Body of Christ,
animated by the Spirit, she is necessary for salvation — but
this necessity is not the same as being "inside" or "outside" her boundaries.

The Church and the kingdom of God

To conclude our review of the Church it is important for
our theme to consider, even if only cursorily, her relationship with the kingdom of God. Throughout the history of
the Church, the two have sometimes been identified,[28] but
in the light of modern scholarship such identification is not
acceptable.

It is clear that the kingdom of God formed the central
theme of the preaching and activity of Jesus.[29] It was for
this that he came on earth: "to preach the gospel of the
kingdom" (Mt 4:23), and it was with this category that he
began his public life: "The time is fulfilled, and the kingdom
of God is at hand; repent, and believe in the gospel" (Mk
1:15). In this powerfully rich symbol of the kingdom rooted
in the Old Testament, Jesus chose to articulate his mission
to the world. In order to understand what he himself thought
of the kingdom we have to delve into the many usages he
made of the expression, for he never defined it as such.
Through the witness of his words and actions, his preaching
and his miracles, but above all through the witness of his
own atoning death and resurrection, Jesus proclaimed that
the God of the kingdom was none other than the Lord of
the universe and that in him, Jesus of Nazareth, the
kingdom and the rule of God had broken upon the world

– a kingdom that meant the saving presence of God, a presence that destroys evil and brings the rule of peace and justice.

The God of the kingdom proclaimed by Jesus is a God who invites all to share in his life, his peace, a God who forgives, a God who urges us to call him, "Abba, Father," – a Father who is grace, love and compassion, a Father prodigal with his mercy and forgiveness; a God who breaks down barriers, who wants to include all within his embrace, sinners and just, the poor and the rich, Jew and Gentile, slave and free. For that reason, the kingdom proclaimed by Jesus has a profoundly universalist tendency, a universalism that tends to destroy the obstacles posed by hatred, enmity, exclusion. For Jesus, the "People of God" is not the "remnant" of the Pharisees or the Essenes but is the whole people, the "Twelve". All are invited to the joyful banquet of the kingdom. Nobody, except those who themselves refuse the invitation, is excluded from it. Jesus sometimes praised the response of those who were thought to be outside the People, as, for example, the centurion (Mt 8:5–13) and the daughter of the Syrophoenician woman (Mk 7:24–30). The inhabitants of Tyre and Sidon will not be judged more strictly than those of Israel itself. Jesus emphasized that what is important is sincerity, authenticity and mercy. He himself stands as a prophetic challenge to all that would tend to be exclusive, closing the entry doors except for "members only". Through his healing ministry, Jesus underlines the fact that the God of the kingdom calls the poor, the weak, the marginalized of society to participation in it – and this ministry was not confined to members of the Jewish race alone. It was given also to Samaritans and Gentiles.

In his preaching, Jesus did not specify when the kingdom will come to its full realization. Sometimes one gets the impression that for him it was imminent (e.g., Mk 1:14–15); at other times it would seem to lie in the distant future (Mt 13:24–30). This same ambiguity is found in the early Church. However, it can be argued that this was demanded by the very nature of the kingdom, for the kingdom is not so much a point of history as a quality of life. For that reason it carries in a remarkable way the double aspect of the "already" and the "not yet". The "already" by the fact that it is, in Christ, now inaugurated, now present; the "not yet" by virtue of the fact that it still awaits its fulfilment in glory.

Between the kingdom foretold by the prophets in the Old Testament, inaugurated by Jesus here on earth, and its entry into fullness in glory, stands the Church. The Church is not the kingdom but in her "the powers of God's kingdom are already operative."[30] Through the Church the risen Lord continues to exercise all his authority and power; through the Church he continues his proclamation of the kingdom, making it present here on earth. The time of the Church is the "era of Christ's hidden rule which in turn is to prepare the way for and bring about the manifestation of the perfect cosmic kingdom of God."[31] Like the kingdom itself, the Church also shares in its aspects of "already" and "not yet" that makes her strive for an ever greater fidelity, ever greater purification of herself, constantly removing the obstacles to the coming of the kingdom. Her prayer is always "Thy kingdom come!"

It is the "already" that makes the Good News always *good* – good for each and every man, woman and child of each generation throughout the whole world; it is the "not yet" that makes the Good News always *new*, something that must always be sought, always lying in the future, always being discovered, always surprising us. The tension formed by the two aspects enables us to enter into dialogue with peoples, cultures, religions everywhere, for in true dialogue there must be mutual sharing, mutual seeking for the fullness to which we are all called. There must be openness and generosity in sharing with others all that we have received and at the same time humble, sensitive listening to what they have received. In the mission of the Church there is never any need for fear in encountering our brothers and sisters of other religions for the seed of the kingdom has been planted in the hearts of *all* mankind and the one criterion that has been given to us for the sifting of the chaff from that seed is Jesus Christ, *the* truth.

Because of the centrality of the figure of Jesus the early Church tended to call the kingdom of God, the kingdom of his Christ. So that, while the kingdom of God is indeed *theo*centric precisely because it is the kingdom of God, God has entrusted it to his Christ, and in Christ it is perfectly signified and effected. For that reason, Christ is the sacrament of the kingdom, and in this sense it is *Christo*centric. Jesus, through his death and exaltation in glory, is now the Lord, the *Kyrios*, and it is through him, and only through him, that salvation is to be achieved, for only in him has humanity been taken into the divinity. For that reason, no other name than that of *"Kyrios"* has been given to man whereby he can be saved. Jesus is Lord, endowed with all authority in heaven and on earth (Mt 28:18).

Like Christ, the Church too must be the sign and instrument of the kingdom here on earth. To put it in another way, if Jesus is the Archsacrament, the *Ursacrament*, of the kingdom of God, then the Church, because of her relationship with Christ and in virtue of the fact that he has poured out his Spirit on her, must also be the sign and instrument of the kingdom here on earth.

> After Easter and the descent of the Holy Spirit, Christ's new community of salvation comes to effective life. With this God's rule rises to a higher level. Jesus is now the Lord, raised to God's right hand, and he directs his Church on earth through his Spirit, and wishes by its means to win mankind for God's reign and kingdom.[32]

In the one economy of salvation, the one God is present, Father, Son and Holy Spirit. It is important to keep this Trinitarian perspective ever in mind. We have already referred to it earlier but here we recall it in relation to the kingdom of God — it is the kingdom of the God who is Trinity and this means that the activity of the Risen Lord is always in and through his Spirit:

> Yet, the action of the Risen Lord — inside and outside the boundaries of the Christian fold — passes in all cases through the Spirit; in the resurrection of Jesus, the Spirit of God has

become the Spirit of Christ. Consequently, every belonging
to the kingdom of God – whether inside or outside the Christian fold – implies a double reference, to Christ and his Spirit.
On the other hand, just as in the Prologue of the Fourth Gospel
the "Word of God" is viewed as universal agent of God's self-
manifestation throughout human history, transcendent to and
independent of his becoming man in Jesus Christ, so too the
Spirit of God is universally present and operative throughout
salvation history, independent of and prior to the Christ
event.[33]

Keeping in mind the presence of the Spirit in the plan of
salvation helps us to understand the relationship between
the Church and other religions. We must not forget that,
as we read in the Acts of the Apostles, "The gift of the Holy
Spirit had been poured out even on the Gentiles" (10:45).
Irenaeus has called the Word and the Spirit, the "two hands
of the Father".[34] Georges Khodr, referring to this phrase,
writes:

> This means that we must affirm not only their hypostatic
> independence but also that the advent of the Holy Spirit in
> the world is not subordinated to the Son, is not simply a
> function of the Word. . . Between the two economies there
> is a reciprocity and a mutual service. The Spirit is another
> Paraclete. . . The Spirit operates and applies his energies in
> accordance with his own economy and we could, from this
> angle, regard the non-Christian religions as points where his
> inspiration is at work.[35]

Seeing the Church in the perspective of the kingdom of
God has important repercussions for our thinking on the
Church. First of all, it underlines that the goal of all her
activity lies not in herself but in the kingdom. The Church
does not exist primarily to make people members of herself
but to make them members of the kingdom, not to make
them Church people but kingdom people. Of course, the
Church hopes that all its members will be kingdom people
and as such she will be truly Church, truly a way to the
kingdom, but just as all Church people are not automatically
guaranteed by virtue of their explicit Church membership
to be also kingdom people, so likewise, not all non-Church

people will, in virtue of that fact, be excluded from the kingdom. The kingdom perspective is broader than that of Church, more inclusive.

Secondly, the kingdom perspective reminds us of the theocentrism of salvation, but a theocentrism that is also Christocentric because Christ is at the centre of the salvation process and this is the way God has willed it. Thus, strictly speaking, there is no dichotomy between Christ and the Church, for salvation is ecclesiocentric only because of the presence of Christ and of his Spirit within the Church.

Thirdly, the kingdom of God underlines in a powerful way the tension between the present and the future — allowing us to have confidence in the present, to value it, but knowing that the future realization of the kingdom will infinitely surpass our understanding and our expectations. We live in a world marked by so many problems: disease, famine, war, violence and evil of all sorts, but at the same time there is a striving for good, for peace, for justice, for equality among all peoples, for love, for greater humanity, and all this striving is the material which the Lord will take to himself and transform into his kingdom. *Gaudium et Spes* puts it this way:

> For after we have obeyed the Lord, and in his Spirit nurtured on earth the values of human dignity, brotherhood and freedom, and indeed all the good fruits of our nature and enterprise, we will find them again, but freed of strain, burnished and transfigured. This will be so when Christ hands over to the Father a kingdom eternal and universal: "a kingdom of truth and life, of holiness and grace, of justice, love, and peace." On this earth that kingdom is already present in mystery. When the Lord returns it will be brought into full flower (No. 39).

We can never define the Church, for the simple reason that you can never define a mystery. The mystery is always greater than any description of it. Even as a sociological entity it is difficult to express.

> The Church is a concept as difficult to put into words as is that of "home". Superficially we tend to identify both with physical edifices but that is not it. There is a story of a

little boy who lived temporarily with his family in a hotel. One day someone said to him: "I see that you live here because you have not yet got a home of your own." "Not at all," the boy replied, "I have a home", and he pointed to his father and mother and brothers and sisters, "but we do not yet have a house to put our home in."[36]

But, if there were one word that describes the "why" of the Church, then that word must be "mission" and it is to this that we now turn.

NOTES

1. Xavier Rynne, *The Second Session* (Faber and Faber, London 1963), p. 354.

2. Edward Schillebeeckx, *World and Church* (Sheed and Ward, London 1971), p. 91.

3. *Ibid.*, pp. 91–92.

4. *Ibid.*

5. Cf. Alexandre Ganoczy, *An Introduction to Catholic Sacramental Theology* (English translation: Paulist Press, New York/Ramsey 1984), pp. 7–30.

6. Henri de Lubac, *Catholicism*, (Burns, Oates and Washbourne, London 1950), p. 29.

7. Karl Rahner, "The Church and Atheism", *Theological Investigations* Vol XXI, p. 142.

8. Vatican I: Schema, chapter 7.

9. Gustave Martelet, "The Church as Sacrament", in *Theological Digest* Vol. 22, No 1 (1974), p. 62.

10. William of Saint-Thierry, *On the Sacrament of the Altar*, (c. 12.; P.L., clxxx, 361–2) quoted by Henri de Lubac, in *Catholicism*, p. 245.

11. Boniface Willems, "Who belongs to the Church", *Concilium* Vol. 1/1 (January 1965), p. 70.

12. Karl Rahner, "The Church and Atheism", *Theological Investigations* Vol XXI, p. 143.

13. Bernard Häring, *The Sacraments in a Secular Age* (St Paul Publications, Slough) *The Sacraments and Your Everyday Life*, (Liguori Publications, Missouri 1976), p. 30.

14. Gustave Martelet, "The Church as Sacrament", p. 63.

15. *De moribus ecclesiae*, chapter 30.

16. *Letter to the Smyrnaeans* 8, 2.

17. E. Zoghby, "Unité et diversité de l'Église", in G. Baraúna (ed.), *L'Église de Vatican II* (Cerf, Paris 1967), Vol. 2, pp. 499–500.

18. *Ibid.*, p. 500.

19. Yves Congar, *The Mystery of the Church* (Chapman, London 1965), p. 101.

20. *Lumen Gentium*, 13.
21. Hans Küng, *The Church* (Sheed and Ward, New York 1967), p. 344.
22. *Letter to the Trallians*, Inscript.
23. *Gaudium et Spes*, 40.
24. *Lumen Gentium*, 16; *Ad Gentes*, 7; *Gaudium et Spes*, 22.
25. Karl Barth, *Church Dogmatics* Vol. 1, Part 2,(T. & T. Clark, Edinburgh 1956), p. 298.
26. *Unitatis Redintegratio* (Decree on Ecumenism), 6.
27. *Lumen Gentium*, 9.
28. E.g., by Augustine (cf. *De Civitate Dei* XX, 9) and Gregory the Great (P.L., LXXVI, col. 32).
29. For a full discussion of the theme see Rudolf Schnackenburg, *God's Rule and Kingdom* (Herder and Herder, New York and Burns and Oates, London, 1963). His book, *The Church in the New Testament* (Herder and Herder, New York and Burns and Oates, London 1965) is also relevant. See also: *Your Kingdom Come*. Report on the World Conference on Mission and Evangelism, Melbourne, May 1980 (World Council of Churches, Geneva 1980).
30. R. Schnackenburg, *God's Rule and Kingdom*, p. 351.
31. *Ibid.,* p. 353.
32. *Ibid.,* p. 381.
33. Jacques Dupuis, "The Kingdom of God and World Religions", in *Vidyajyoti* 51 (November 1987), p. 539.
34. Cf. *Adv. Haer.* IV, ch. xx, 1.
35. Georges Khodr, "Christianity in a Pluralistic World – the Economy of the Holy Spirit", in *The Ecumenical Review* XXIII, No. 2 (1971), p. 126.
36. Metropolitan Emilianos, "Urgent Need of a Common Mission", in *International Review of Mission*, Vol. LXXII, No. 286 (April 1983), pp. 260–261.

6

Mission

The Church founded by Jesus Christ came to realize very
early on that its mission was the same as that of his own
and, like his, that this involved breaking out of the barriers imposed by race and culture, language and religion,
– that it was universal in every sense of the term. Now,
since the Christian mission is the continuation of the mission of Christ, then as such it has its origin in the heart of
God himself, in his gracious decision to share his love, his
life with other created beings, a decision he implemented
in his work of creation and the history of salvation and
which found its greatest expression and effectiveness in the
life, death and resurrection of Jesus Christ. The whole
Bible is therefore a witness to this mission of God, this
sending forth of his loving invitation to mankind to share
his life, and man's response to that invitation. Another way
of putting it is to say that the whole Bible is a witness to
God's salvific will to save every human being who enters
into this world.

It would be instructive to look at all the Bible from a missionary viewpoint[1] but here I will confine my remarks to
some aspects of the missionary perspective of the New Testament, looking briefly at Paul, the Synoptics, John and the
authors of 1 Peter and Revelation. We will try to see how
these New Testament witnesses understood the mission
which they had received from Jesus Christ.

Paul

The Damascus experience of Paul brought home to him
in a powerful way that the Good News of Jesus Christ was
for the whole world. In virtue of his dramatic encounter
with the Risen Lord (three times recounted in his Letters:

Gal 1:11–17; 1 Cor 15:8–11; 9:1–2.), Paul received the profound conviction that Jesus, the Crucified One, the Messiah, had been raised from the dead, and therefore the salvation of all humanity could only be achieved in and through him. Because of the resurrection of the Crucified One (and this was the supreme image of Paul's focus on the earthly Jesus), God's plan of salvation has entered its final, definitive stage. Everything else in Paul stems from this conviction. If the one God of all peoples offers salvation to everyone without distinction, to Gentiles as to Jews, through the mediation of Jesus Christ (Rom 1:16–17; 3:21–30; 1 Thess 5:9) then it follows that the "chosen people" is not the Israel of the flesh but the "Israel of God" (Gal 6: 16). Likewise, if Jesus is the promised and long-awaited Messiah, the Son of God, the instrument which God extends to humanity for its salvation, then the obvious deduction is that the messianic age has broken upon us and the road to the kingdom is now through Jesus – he is the very road itself, the Way, and there is no other – and, therefore, he, the Good News, must be announced immediately. This final stage of God's plan is therefore in a special way the age of mission, an age which Paul saw confirmed by the pouring of the Spirit on the communities. For Paul, what Jesus said and did during his life here on earth are not so vitally important as the fact of who Jesus *is*; and his death and resurrection is the kernel, the keystone to the understanding of who Jesus is and, therefore, the heart of the Good News as proclaimed by Paul. This profound conviction of who Jesus is was the motive force of all Paul's activity, that which urged him to evangelize no matter what the cost to himself. It was this same sense of urgency that made him cry out in anguish: "Woe to me if I do not preach the gospel!" (1 Cor 9:16; cf. 2 Cor 5:16–20; Rom 10:12–15; 15:15–21). He is deeply conscious that he is an *apostle*, one *sent* by none other than God himself, to proclaim the Good News of Jesus Christ, and more particularly one sent to the Gentiles.

Because of Paul's profound conviction of this truth, because of the coherence with which he followed it through and because of its Christocentrism, no one contributed as

Paul did to the articulation of the understanding of the Christian mission – a mission which he himself, in the Letters to the Colossians and to the Ephesians, will extend so as to embrace the whole of the cosmos. He wants to communicate to all his own experience of the universal reconciliation brought about by God in and through Jesus Christ at whose service he now places all his energies. He is deeply aware that in Christ God irrupted on the world in a new and marvellous way and therefore *now* is the time when "the righteousness of God has been manifested" (Rom 3:21), "*now* is the acceptable time; behold, now is the day of salvation" (2 Cor 6:2). In Christ time has broken in on eternity and all humanity is called to respond to God. The Church is the medium through which this call is made.

The Synoptics

The Gospels, too, articulate this conviction of being sent by God to announce the Good News to the whole world. The Synoptic writers realize that they are communicating a *Gospel*, a "Good *spel*", a "Good story or news", and, as such, it demands proclamation. Good news must be so for someone, otherwise it is meaningless. Unproclaimed good news is a contradiction in terms. Only the deep conviction of how wonderfully good the Good News is will initiate and sustain mission.

Mark presents Jesus as making a journey from Galilee to Jerusalem, always on the move proclaiming the kingdom which is close at hand, which is coming. Matthew follows basically the same pattern, amplifying it somewhat with the inclusion of the infancy narrative and some important discourses. Luke, with a more explicit consciousness of the universalist implications of the message of Jesus, presents these right at the very beginning. Jesus is the salvation which God had prepared for all the nations to see, ". . . mine eyes have seen thy salvation which thou hast prepared in the presence of all peoples, a light for revelation to the Gentiles and a glory to thy people Israel" (Lk 2:30–32). His journey to Jerusalem is necessary, for he had to suffer,

"Thus it is written that the Christ should suffer and on the third day rise from the dead, and that repentance and forgiveness of sins should be preached in his name to all nations, beginning from Jerusalem" (Lk 24:46–47). For the three Synoptics, the death and resurrection of Jesus proclaim his authority and the paschal mystery is the fundamental departure point for the universal mission.

However, unlike Paul, for the Synoptics the pre-paschal Jesus is also significant for the understanding of the Christian mission. In telling of his life, his preaching, his relationship with the men and women whom he met on his journey, his liberating actions on their behalf, his interpretation of the Law – all are inviting his followers, his disciples, those who believe in him, to be inspired by him, by his life, for only in this way can they continue his mission here on earth, only by immersion in the Spirit of Christ, in him, can we be sure that we are proclaiming him and not ourselves, evangelizing as he evangelized. For the first three evangelists, the mission of the Church is a liberating mission which has its source in the kingdom of God proclaimed and inaugurated in Jesus; and the manner or style in which this mission is to be performed is none other than the manner and style of Jesus himself. This means that Christian mission, if it is to be like that of Christ himself, must go first to the most needy, to the poor, the weak, the despised, the marginalized but at the same time no one is to be excluded. All three Synoptics emphasize the centrality of the kingdom and the attitude of Jesus toward it and toward those called to be members of it – his compassion, his acceptance of people, his liberty – and in this way they show that he is the saviour of the world. The Christian mission has no frontiers, nor can it have, because Christ took all humanity to himself in the Incarnation and he died for all humanity.

Each evangelist brings this truth out, each in his own way. Mark has the mission of Jesus spreading out, as it were, in concentric circles, "first to the Jews" (7:27–29) and then to "all the nations" (13:10). Those who may have regarded themselves as the rightful heirs to the kingdom by right of birth are sometimes rejected while those who have been marginalized, excluded, are accepted. For Matthew, Jesus is the focal point of all history. In him all the past comes to its culmination and the final definitive era is inaugurated. There is in him an expectation of the imminent end and this must spur us on to ever greater charity (cf. chapters 24 and 25). It is, however, in Luke that the most emphatic expression of the universal nature of Christ's mission is to be found, especially if we take his *Acts* as the second volume of his Gospel. For him the mission of Jesus continued in the Church is a mission which spreads out from Jerusalem to Judaea and Samaria and then to the ends of the earth (cf. Acts 1:8; Lk 24:47).

The three evangelists likewise underline the fact that the mission of Jesus is passed on to his disciples. They are called to be "fishers of men" (Mt 4:19; Mk 1:17), sent as he himself was sent. To be a true disciple is to obey him in action, in one's life — it is to live as he did, to live a life of love. His disciples are to be his "witnesses" — witnesses to all he said, all he did, all that he is. Luke adverts us to the fact that the liberating work of God proclaimed in Jesus is now confided to weak, sinful, human beings. Because of this, the power to perform the mission comes not from ourselves but from the Risen Lord who constantly pours out his Spirit upon the Church and to whom is given all authority in heaven and on earth. This mission of Jesus is one that is ever tending towards the formation of communities - communities united in faith, in hope and in love, communities that maintain themselves open to all who wish to respond to the Lord's invitation and who never close in upon themselves.

And they devoted themselves to the apostles' teaching and fellowship, to the breaking of bread and the prayers. (Acts 2:42)

In this verse Luke sums up what being a Christian community means: a community gathered around the bread of the Word and the bread of the Eucharist; a community that manifests itself in fellowship and prayer. The formation of such communities is the goal of all Christian mission.

Because their centre is Christ, sacramentally present in the Eucharist, we can call them Eucharistic communities. Whatever our Christian missionary activities are they must have this as their ultimate aim. Whether we are in young parishes or simple mission stations, whether we are in schools, hospitals, seminaries or houses of formation, the creation and building up of Eucharistic communities must be our aim, each one contributing according to the gifts and abilities he or she has received.

We repeat: what sustains, directs and vitalizes the mission of the Church is none other than the Holy Spirit. The Spirit, as it were, replaces Jesus in the midst of the communities or, rather, the risen Christ is present to them in and through the Spirit. *Acts* in particular underlines this aspect of the Christian mission. The Spirit is the catalyst within the community, ever calling it forth to fulfil its vocation, giving it the necessary strength, courage and power to do so. He is the bond which unites the history of Jesus to the history of the community, the mission of Jesus to the mission of the community. That is why Pentecost rather than being the birthday of the Church is the proclamation of the mission of the Church — a mission which brings down the barriers and divisions within humanity, symbolized in the proclamation's transcending the multiplicity of languages (Acts 2:8).

John

John does not use the symbol of the "kingdom of God" in order to articulate his understanding of the Christian mission but he does use other symbols which are not specifically Jewish but rather universal: bread, light, water, life, road, truth, resurrection. These are symbols which can be understood by peoples throughout the whole world. For John, Jesus is the "Son of man" who reveals the universal love of God — a revelation that takes place above all in the Cross, the supreme moment of love, the supreme manifestation of the self-giving of God, of the mission of Jesus. In the Cross we discover the depths of God's love for humanity, a love that is nothing less than God making himself responsible for our happiness, identifying himself with our needs, our misery, our wretchedness. The Cross is the revelation of the mercy of God, his putting his heart alongside human misery. For that reason Jesus is the "saviour of the world" (Jn 4:42), he is the "light of the world" (8:12; 9:5), "the Lamb of God who takes away the sin of the world" (1:29) "the living bread, come down from heaven . . . for the life of the world" (6:51). Jesus is the living presence of God on earth and as such responds to the deepest longings of mankind, the deepest desires of each individual man or woman.

Like the Synoptics, John also emphasizes that the disciples have the same mission as their Master: "As the Father has sent me, even so I send you" (20:21). In order to fulfil its mission, therefore, the Christian community must be like Christ, for only in this way can it too be the "light of the world", the "salt of the earth", the "leaven in the mass" (cf. 1:14–18; 3:16–17; 6:38–40; 12:44–47). The world is the world of men and women and as such it is the object of God's love (3:16–17); but precisely because it is the world of men and women — that is, a world of personal, free, human beings — then the world can also reject the offer of God's love. The Christian mission, therefore, is called upon to offer this love, to proclaim the invitation to share in it. Furthermore, it is within this love, within this invitation that the mission itself arises, that it is born and moves. For that reason missionary zeal and activity need not despair, nor flag, nor become discouraged before the rejections and difficulties which it inevitably encounters. Jesus himself lived and suffered these contradictions — and triumphed over them. The Church cannot expect otherwise as regards the problems but because of Christ she can be confident of the ultimate victory. A Christian is one who knows that life is stronger than death no matter what its manifestations; knows that love is stronger than hate no matter how virulently this latter may manifest itself; knows that he can hope in an unlimited way, a hope that gives patience in awaiting the Coming of the Lord, that gives a tremendous liberty from any sense of self-sufficiency for all our trust in the saving power of God through Christ.

1 Peter and Revelation

In these two documents we have an important missionary perspective. They do not present the origin of the missionary vocation so much in the salvific plan of God itself but rather in Baptism and the Christian vocation. The Christian is the one *chosen*, the one who has come into a magnificent heritage:

> Blessed be the God and Father of our Lord Jesus Christ! By his great mercy we have been born anew to a living hope through the resurrection of Jesus Christ from the dead, and to an inheritance which is imperishable, undefiled, and unfading, kept in heaven for you, who by God's power are guarded through faith for a salvation ready to be revealed in the last time. (1 Pet 1:3–5)

He is the one who has been purified in the waters of Baptism and for that reason he can jump with joy because of the hope that is in him and justify that hope before others (3:15). It does not matter that the community is small or that it is despised, that it is opposed or even persecuted — what is important is that it witnesses to the living hope within it. Only in this way will the new heaven and the new earth be ushered in, when all will be renewed, transformed, freed from all opposition and corruption:

> I saw no temple in the city, for its temple is the Lord God the Almighty and the Lamb. And the city has no need of sun or moon to shine upon it, for the glory of God is its light, and its lamp is the Lamb. By its light shall the nations walk; and the kings of the earth shall bring their glory into it, and its gates shall never be shut by day — and there shall be no night there; they shall bring into it the glory and the honour of the nations. (Rev 21:22–26)

The two authors remind us that we are a future-oriented people, called to collaborate in the building of a new world, a world of universal peace and brotherhood, a world of justice and equality between all human beings. Christ is ahead of us, leading the way, calling us forward. To believe is to respond to that call.

> The proclamation of the resurrection of Jesus, which can never be separated from the message of the crucifixion, is essentially a proclamation of promise which initiates the Christian mission. This mission achieves its future in so far as the Christian alters and "innovates" the world towards that future of God which is definitely promised to us in the resurrection of Jesus Christ.[2]

The Church is missionary

In this rapid survey of the New Testament basis for the Christian mission, I think we can see why the Second Vatican Council declared that:

> The pilgrim Church is missionary of her very nature. For it is from the mission of the Son and the mission of the Holy Spirit that she takes her origin, in accordance with the decree of God the Father.[3]

Since then this idea has been repeated many times, so often in fact that it runs the risk of becoming trite and misunderstood. It does not, for example, mean that because the whole Church is missionary there is no need for the "professional" missionary, the "foreign" missionary. Such would be a complete misinterpretation of the mind of the Council. What the Council wanted to do was to bring the mission of the Church into the centre of her being. The "missions" had become a "wing" of the Church's activity, something that was almost peripheral, something to which a few people were called but which did not really concern the vast majority of believers. The Council wanted the whole Church to see herself from the perspective of mission and in this perspective all else was to be evaluated — her institutions, her different activities, her preaching, her witness. The Church is Church in the measure in which she fulfils the service to which she is called, in the measure in which she evangelizes. Pope John Paul II repeated this in his opening address to the Latin American bishops gathered in Puebla on 12 February 1979:

. . . evangelization is the essential mission, the distinctive vocation and the deepest identity of the Church which has in turn been evangelized.

For this reason, the declaration that the whole Church is missionary does not in any way diminish the importance of the "professional" or "foreign" missionary. On the contrary, it intensifies it. We might compare it to a declaration that the whole Church must be a praying Church. No one would think that such a declaration would in any way diminish the importance of the contemplative charism but would rather see in it a call for that charism to be intensified. The more the call to prayer is lived in a radical way, the more does the whole Church become aware of the importance of prayer. So likewise, the more the missionary nature of the Church is manifested in a radical way, in the actual going out to evangelize, in the actual leaving of one's home and country to do so, then so much the more will the whole Church become aware of its missionary obligation and respond to it. The different charisms of the Church interact and complement one another.

The physical leaving of one's own home and fatherland to announce the Good News of Jesus Christ underlines the fact that the faith we have received is a gift to be shared, a gift given to us not primarily for ourselves and our own well-being but for the good of others. That is why mission must become the spontaneous expression of what it means to be a Christian, what it means to be a disciple of Christ, to take him at his word, to accept the Good News that he has proclaimed and that we believe, news that is truly and always good, that is relevant to our lives here on earth in this present time, that is meaningful for us, and not just for us but is relevant and meaningful for the whole world. To be a disciple of Christ is to be his witness in the world, to be his missionary, and we are missionary in the measure in which we are his disciples. It is to follow Christ, the One sent, the missionary of the Father, sent by him "to preach good news to the poor . . . to proclaim release to the captives and recovering of sight to the blind'' (Lk 4:18).

As already mentioned, the mission of the Church must be performed in and through the Spirit of Jesus Christ, for it is only in this Spirit that it will truly be a Christian mission, and that means in effect that only *love* can be its foundation, only love can be its motive force, the dynamism behind it, the life which animates it. Because of this there is no room for proselytism, no room for coercion of any sort — be it cultural, economic, political or otherwise. The method and the approach of the Christian missionary can only be those of Christ, who came into the world in order to identify with mankind, who became incarnate in this world, who became all things to all men. It means accepting the truth that the weakness of love is the strength of the missionary and that any other ''strength'' — money, influence, prestige, power, authority, etc. — is indeed weakness. The Christian missionary is one convinced that in dying we find life, in giving that we receive, in emptying ourselves we become full of God. This is a difficult lesson to learn, a difficult example to imitate. Time after time we discover the ''world'' — in its negative connotation — in us, the presence of sin, sin that is egoism, selfishness, sin in the singular, sin that is hostility towards God and his reign, the reluctance to trust God, to believe in any other power than our own. Despite all the examples in the history of the Church, in the history of her mission, we find it hard to believe that giving ourselves in love — even if this means actual death — is the greatest source of life. For that reason the Cross stands at the heart of missionary spirituality. The Cross stands as the supreme manifestation of God's love for us, the supreme word of God to man of his solidarity with us, his commitment to our happiness, and so it is the central missionary commission. His ''Go and make disciples of all nations . . .'' is but the expression of the commission already implied in the Cross. ''This is my commandment, that you love one another *as* I have loved you (Jn 15:12).'' It is only in the light of the Cross that this commandment can be understood.[4]

It is of vital importance that all of this be taken into account particularly in today's world, for it cannot be denied that in recent times the concept of "missions" has come in for some severe criticism — under the headings of "imperialism", "colonialism", "paternalism", "intolerance", "inauthenticity". And no doubt, because of aspects of our past, such criticism is not completely unjustified. We cannot really be surprised if some see in Christian mission of the last few hundred years aspects of European and North American triumphalism and imperialism — the attempt to impose on other people their concept of "what is good for them", where everything is judged from a definite ethnocentrism and where the values and cultures of other peoples are seen as inferior, dehumanizing, if not downright demonic. Can the expansion of the Church in Latin America not be seen as a continuation of the *reconquista* mentality? And even though we distinguish between political society and the Church community, nevertheless it should not surprise us if some would claim that the same mentality can be found in both — a mentality characterized by conquest, even if within the Church this is expressed as the "conquest" of souls for Christ.

Associated with this imperialism is the accusation against the Church of being guilty of a "colonial" mentality. It is true that the modern missionary movement coincided with the colonial period and very often the missionary was seen as the "spiritual" arm of the colonial powers, one of the famous — or infamous — three "M"'s: the Merchant, the Military and the Missionary. Some would argue that now that the colonial era is over the missionary should go, for, they claim, true independence will not be achieved until the last missionary has left, for whether we like it or not, the missionary shares in the general discredit of colonialism. Very often, the longing for full world citizenship, complete independence — economic, educational, cultural as well as political — is accompanied by a certain resentment, antagonism against all visible expressions of colonialism — and this even within the ecclesial field. For this reason, the missionary may sometimes feel unwanted, feel that his presence is resented, despite official statements to the contrary.

A third attitude that is resented is that of paternalism. For many years the missionary took decisions, "solved" problems for people — very often without consulting them, without presuming that they could have something to contribute to the case in hand — so that when the change took place many were still dependent on the "know-how" of the missionary, on his pastoral expertise, on his economic, educational and organization skills. This may have been permissible right at the very beginning (and even then it is debatable) but now it is an obstacle to growth. It is preventing the Church in those countries from coming to full maturity, hindering its normal development.

These and such like criticisms which form part of the normal day-to-day life of the missionary on the field must not be seen as a call to abandon the mission but rather as a call from the Spirit to re-examine one's own missionary attitudes and presuppositions, a call to purify one's approach of all sense of superiority, all attempts to coerce. It means being conscious of the ever-present call to conversion, to listen to the Good News, allow oneself to be constantly purified by it, constantly evangelized. That is why the new approach is often called the dialogical approach; but this is none other than the approach of Christ himself, the approach of the Spirit, who entered into dialogue with humanity from within, as it were, rather than from without, with humility, respect, sensitivity — in a word, with love.

It is in this light that the mission of the Church must always be seen. This must be her relationship with all, including the followers of other religions. In the light which is Christ there is no room for arrogance, no room for a superiority complex, but only humble respect as one enters into dialogue with people of living faiths, searching with them for the full truth of salvation and what it means for all of us here and now in our different existential situations. This searching together demands humility and generosity, openness and commitment. We must have the humility to recognize and accept that we do not possess the fullness of the truth of Jesus Christ; that God speaks to me normally through the people and circumstances of my daily life who too are seeking in the Spirit for the same fullness. Through them the Spirit can awaken in me awareness of elements of my own tradition to which I was hitherto unaware. For that reason we need humility to listen to one another, to listen not only with one's intelligence but also with one's heart, to listen sensitively, from within the other's perspective in so far as that is possible. Only in this way can one discover what the Spirit has revealed to them regarding the one process of salvation that has been made manifest. God normally speaks to us, reveals to us the ever emerging fullness of the kingdom for which we long, in and through the historical process, in and through the experiences and encounters of one's life.

It also demands, as I have said, commitment and generosity, generosity to give and share all that I am and have, all that I am committed to, and that includes the deepest conviction of one's life, that which gives meaning to one's whole existence, one's faith. It would be a poor sort of dialogue if I were not prepared to share with my partners what it is that I live by, what it is that makes me "tick". It would be like going to another in order to have a conversation with him/her and then on arrival refusing to open one's mouth.

In its Declaration on Religious Liberty, the Second Vatican Council said:

Truth, however, is to be sought after in a manner proper to the dignity of the human person and his social nature. The inquiry is to be free, carried on with the aid of teaching or instruction, communication, and dialogue. In the course of these, men explain to one another the truth they have discovered, or think they have discovered, in order thus to assist one another in the quest for truth. Moreover, as the truth is discovered, it is by a personal assent that men are to adhere to it. (No. 3)

And in No. 4 we find the following:

However, in spreading religious faith and in introducing religious practices, everyone ought at all times to refrain from any manner of action which might seem to carry a hint of coercion or of a kind of persuasion that would be dishonourable or unworthy, especially when dealing with poor or uneducated people. Such a manner of action would have to be considered an abuse of one's own right and a violation of the right of others.

John Paul II tells us that "man is the first path which the Church ought to traverse in carrying out its mission" (*Redemptor Hominis*, 14). In the same document we find an important statement with relevance to Christian mission:

> This man is the way for the Church . . . because man — every man without any exception whatever — has been re- deemed by Christ, and because with man — with each man without any exception whatever — Christ is in a way united, even when man is unaware of it: "Christ, who died and was raised up for all, provides man" — each man and every man — "with all the light and the strength to measure up to his supreme calling".

One might ask, but what about conversion? Are mis- sionaries no longer to strive to bring about the conversion of others to the one true Church of Jesus Christ? The answer is, yes. But conversion must be understood properly. Con- version is not first and foremost the changing from one religion to another — that may well be an aspect of con- version but does not form its essence. Indeed, a change from one religion to another may take place without there being any true conversion. Conversion essentially is the turning of one's whole person to God in order to submit oneself ever more completely, ever more generously to him and to his will. This however, because of man's social nature, will strive for realization within the bosom of a community and, in this sense, conversion to God will also entail, normally, conversion to a religious community, to the Church. The call to conversion is directed not merely to those who are outside the Church but also to those inside, and those who make the call must themselves respond to it. Conversion is not something that is effected once and for all but is rather a constant permanent attitude, an integral part of one's total response to God. Indeed, as has already been pointed out, conversion, repentance, *metanoia*, is the first requirement of the act of faith. It is the turning away from all that is not God in order to unite ourselves more fully with him. In order to proclaim Christ we have to let Christ live in us, allow him to mould us into his likeness, to make our thoughts, our ways of relating to others, our manner of forgiving, conform to him.

In this regard it is important to recall the primacy of conscience. Again Pope John Paul II might be quoted on this point:

> The human person's dignity itself becomes part of the content of the proclamation (of the truth), being included not necessarily in words but by an attitude towards it. This attitude seems to fit the special needs of our times. Since man's true freedom is not found in everything that the various systems and individuals see and propagate as freedom, the Church, because of her divine mission, becomes all the more the guardian of this freedom, which is the condition and basis for the human person's true dignity. (*Redemptor Hominis*, 12)

The agent of conversion is none other than the Holy Spirit, for

> . . . he is the end and the goal of all evangelization. It is he alone who produces that new creation, that is, the new human nature towards which evangelization is striving through that unity in variety which evangelization must necessarily evoke in the Christian community. It is through the Holy Spirit that the Gospel is disseminated throughout the world as it is he alone who reveals the signs of the times — signs willed by God — which evangelization receives and elucidates in the life of men. (Paul VI, *Evangelii Nuntiandi*, 75)

The Holy Spirit will bring all things to their fullness. How and when, we do not know, but we can trust him, and simply obey what he has given us to do: proclaim in love the Good News of Jesus Christ to all nations. Docility to the Spirit is achieved through prayer, that is, immersing oneself in the relationship with God in which we have been inserted through faith in Jesus Christ, experiencing daily the God who loves us, calls us, gives us hope. It is to enter into that communion we celebrate in the Eucharist, and let that communion become transparent in our lives. In the communion with Christ we live the Good News and are thereby capacitated to announce it with courage, confidence and unbounded hope, with joy and peace in our hearts. In celebrating our insertion into Christ's death and resurrection we at the same time proclaim his coming: *Maranatha!* Come, Lord Jesus!

Very often, in the mission fields of Africa and Asia, the Muslim call from the minaret rings out: *"Allahu-Akbar!"* — God is Greater! We Christians too can and must take that call to heart and know that the infinite God and Father of all creation knows how to bring all beings to their fullness, to salvation, in Jesus Christ, his Son, in whom and for whom he created all that exists. God is infinitely greater than our little thoughts.

NOTES

1. Cf. D. Senior/C. Stuhlmueller: *The Biblical Foundations for Mission* (Orbis Books, Maryknoll, N.Y. 1983).

2. Johannes B. Metz, *Theology of the World* (Burns and Oates, London 1969), p. 89.

3. *Ad Gentes*, 2.

4. For a beautiful and profound insight into missionary spirituality, see: Segundo Galilea, *The Beatitudes: To Evangelize as Jesus Did* (Orbis Books, Maryknoll, N.Y. 1984).

EPILOGUE

In the foregoing review of some aspects of the Christian mission in the light of the problem of its relationships to other religions, one becomes very aware of the interconnectedness of the whole of Christianity, the underlying unity of the different elements which constitute God's call to humanity to share his life and man's response to that invitation. One becomes aware of the Mystery — understood as a superabundance of light — that underpins everything, underlies man's very being and existence here on earth, and that even in the beatific vision this Mystery will not be dissolved. Our language at best can only be analogical, a groping or striving to give voice to the incomprehensibility of God. The more one delves into the message of our faith, the more one becomes conscious of the innate tension which is to be found between the different poles of the questions, between God's transcendence and immanence, between nature and grace, grace and freedom, between the "already" and the "not yet", between creation and Incarnation, between the mystery and the sacrament, between the eternal and the temporal, between the Church and the world. The two sides must not be seen as being in mutual opposition. The relationship between the two must not be destroyed in any facile synthesis but rather maintained in creative tension. In that way we do not destroy the unity inherent in God's plan of salvation nor introduce false antinomies, while at the same time we can maintain the fullness of the truth of revelation of God's plan as revealed in Jesus Christ.

In all of this one has to keep in mind that salvation, to be really salvation, must come from outside man and at the same time must be effected from within man. Man unaided is radically incapable of achieving the salvation for which he longs, incapable of escaping the death threat which marks his existence here on earth. This means that salvation fundamentally is something that man can receive only from without. Yet, if it is to be salvation in the true sense of the term it must touch the very centre of man's being, affect his whole nature in all its dimensions. Thus we have the mystery of the Incarnation, that in the one person Jesus Christ we have the two natures, human and divine. Only in him can salvation in the strict sense be effected. The mystery of the Incarnation lies therefore at the heart of the mystery of salvation. And just as we must ever maintain in tension the mystery of the God/Man, falling neither into the heresy of Mani nor that of Pelagius, so likewise we must maintain in tension all the consequent polarities revealed in this mystery. This applies whether we talk about the mystery of salvation as a whole, about the mystery of the revelation of that salvation, about the acceptance of it in faith, the sacramentalization of it in the Church, or the proclamation of it in mission. Far from "mythologizing" the Incarnation, I feel that its reality is essential to the understanding of the mystery of the salvific will of God as manifested in the Church and as present in the world. The Incarnation is not an obstacle to the understanding of the relationship between Christianity and other religions but rather the key to that understanding. The scandal of the Incarnation is what makes understandable the "scandal" of the Church as the necessary instrument of salvation. And just as the coming of Christ to the world meant the liberation of the world, the exaltation of humanity, the breaking of its chains of captivity, the revelation of the dignity of man so, likewise, the coming of the Church — her mission — must have the same significance to the peoples of the world. The fact that this has not always been so nor in all areas of human endeavour does not invalidate her claim but rather calls her to conversion, to purification, to greater fidelity to her Head, to the Spirit within her. The missionary activity of the Church and her relationship with other world religions can only have love as their motive force and it is only by entering into this love relationship, by entering into it through the Spirit of God who is Love, can we discover what it will mean in each and every circumstance. Love alone will give us the required sensitivity, humility, generosity and openness in our outreach to others. Love is the dynamic power of mission, love is its approach, and the fullness of love is its goal.

Select bibliography

Abbott, M. Walter (ed.), *The Documents of Vatican II* (Geoffrey Chapman, London–Dublin, 1966).

Alfaro, J., *Christian Hope and the Liberation of Man* (E. J. Dwyer, Rome and Sydney, 1978).

Anderson, G. H. and Stransky, T. F. (eds), *Christ's Lordship and Religious Pluralism* (Orbis Books, Maryknoll, N.Y., 1981).

Baillie, J., *The Idea of Revelation in Recent Thought* (Columbia University Press, New York, 1956).

Barth, K., *Church Dogmatics* Vol. 1/2 (T. & T. Clark, Edinburgh, 1956).

Brunner, E., *Revelation and Reason* (SCM Press, London/Westminster Press, Philadelphia, 1947).

Bühlmann, W., *The Coming of the Third Church* (St Paul Publications, Slough and Orbis Books, Maryknoll, N.Y., 1977).

— *The Chosen Peoples* (St Paul Publications, Slough and [*God's Chosen Peoples*] Orbis Books, Maryknoll, N.Y., 1983).

— *The Missions on Trial* (St Paul Publications, Slough and Orbis Books, Maryknoll, N.Y., 1979).

— *The Church of the Future. A model for the year 2001.* (St Paul Publications, Slough,/Orbis Books, Maryknoll, N.Y./Dove Communications, Blackburn, Australia, 1986).

Bulst, W., *Revelation* (Sheed & Ward, New York, 1965).

Cobb, J. B., *Christ in a Pluralistic Age* (Westminster Press, Philadelphia, 1975).

Congar, Y., *The Wide World My Parish* (Helicon Press, Baltimore, 1961).

— *The Mystery of the Church* (Chapman, London, 1965).

— *The Revelation of God* (Darton, Longman and Todd, London, 1968).

Coward, H., *Pluralism. Challenge of World Religions* (Orbis Books, Maryknoll, N.Y., 1985).

Cragg, K., *Christianity in World Perspective* (Lutterworth Press, London, 1968).

— *The Christian and Other Religions* (Mowbrays, London, 1977).

Daly, G., *Creation and Redemption* (Gill and Macmillan, Dublin, 1988).

Daniélou, J., *The Salvation of the Nations* (Sheed and Ward, London, 1949).

— *Holy Pagans of the Old Testament* (Sheed and Ward, London, 1957).

— *The Scandal of Truth* (Burns and Oates, London, 1962).

Dawe, D. and Carman, J. (eds), *Christian Faith in a Religiously Plural World* (Orbis Books, Maryknoll, N.Y., 1978).

de Lubac, H., *Catholicism* (Burns and Oates, London, 1950).

Dulles, A., *Revelation Theology* (Burns and Oates, London, 1970).

— *Models of the Church* (Doubleday and Co. Garden City, N.Y., 1974).

— *Models of Revelation* (Doubleday and Co. Garden City, N.Y., 1985).

Dupuis, J., *Jesus Christ and His Spirit* (Theological Publications of India, Bangalore, 1977).

Flanagan, P., (ed.), *A New Missionary Era* (Irish Missionary Union, Dublin, 1979).

Flannery, A., (ed.), *Documents of Vatican II* (Wm. B. Eerdmans Publishing Co., Grand Rapids, Michigan, 1975).

Foy, W., (ed.) *Man's Religious Quest* (Croom Helm, London, 1978).

Select bibliography 131

Fries, H., *Revelation* (Burns & Oates, London and Herder and Herder, New York, 1970).

Galilea, S., *The Beatitudes. To Evangelize as Jesus Did* (Orbis Books, Maryknoll, N.Y., 1984).

Ganoczy, A., *An Introduction to Catholic Sacramental Theology* (Paulist Press, New York/Ramsey, 1984).

Goulder, M. (ed.) *Incarnation and Myth* (SCM, London, 1979).

Green, M. (ed.) *The Truth of God Incarnate* (Hodder and Stoughton, London, 1977).

Griffiths, B., *Return to the Centre* (Collins, London, 1976).

— *The Marriage of East and West* (Collins, London, 1982).

Hacker, P., *Theological Foundations of Evangelization* (Steyler Verlag, St Augustin, 1980).

Hick, J., *God and the Universe of Faiths* (Macmillan, London, 1973).

— *Problems of Religious Pluralism* (Macmillan, London, 1985).

— *God Has Many Names* (Macmillan, London, 1980).

— (ed.) *Truth and Dialogue* (Sheldon Press, London and Westminster Press, Philadelphia, 1974).

— (ed.) *The Myth of God Incarnate* (SCM, London, 1977).

— and Knitter, P., (eds.) *The Myth of Christian Uniqueness* (SCM, London, 1987).

Hillman, E., *The Wider Ecumenism: Anonymous Christianity and the Church* (Burns and Oates, London and Herder and Herder, New York, 1968).

Hocking, W. E., *Living Religions and a World Faith* (Allen and Unwin, London and Macmillan, New York, 1947).

Howard, L., *The Expansion of God* (SCM, London and Orbis Books, Maryknoll, N.Y., 1981).

Inch, M. A., *Doing Theology Across Cultures* (Baker Book House, Michigan, 1982).

Knitter, P. F., *No Other Name?* (Orbis Books, Maryknoll, N.Y., 1985).

Kraemer, H., *The Christian Message in a Non-Christian World* (Harper and Row, New York and Edinburgh House Press, London, 1938).

Küng, H., *The Church* (Herder and Herder, New York/London, 1967).

— *On Being a Christian* (Collins, London, 1977).

— *Does God Exist?* (Collins, London, 1980).

— *Christianity and the World Religions* (Collins Fount, London, 1987).

Moran, G., *Theology and Revelation* (Herder and Herder, New York, 1966).

— *The Present Revelation* (Herder and Herder, New York, 1972).

Müller, K., *Mission Theology. An Introduction* (Steyler Verlag, St Augustin, 1987).

— and Sundermeier, T., (eds.) *Lexikon missionstheologischer Grundbegriffe* (Dietrich Reimer Verlag, Berlin, 1987).

Neill, S., *Christian Faith and Other Faiths* (OUP, Oxford, 1970).

Neuner, J., (ed.) *Christian Revelation and World Religions* (Burns and Oates, London, 1967).

Newbegin, L., *A Faith for this One World?* (SCM, London and Allenson, Naperville, 1961).

— *The Open Secret* (Wm. Eerdmans, Grand Rapids, Michigan, 1978).

Panikkar, R., *The Trinity and World Religions* (Christian Literature Society, Madras, 1970).

— *The Intrareligious Dialogue* (Paulist Press, New York, 1978).

— *The Unknown Christ of Hinduism* (new edition, Darton, Longman and Todd, London, 1981).

Pannenberg, W., *Jesus: God and Man* (Westminster Press, Philadelphia, 1964).

— *Revelation as History* (Sheed and Ward, London, 1969).

— *Faith and Reality* (Search Press, London and Westminster Press, Philadelphia, 1975).

— *Basic Questions in Theology*, 3 vols. (SCM, London, 1973).

Parrinder, G., *Encountering World Religions* (T. & T. Clark, Edinburgh, 1987).
Race, A., *Christians and Religious Pluralism: Patterns in the Christian Theology of Religions* (Orbis Books, Maryknoll, N.Y., 1983).
Rahner, K., *Theological Investigations*, Vol. V (Darton, Longman and Todd, London and Seabury, New York, 1966).
— Vol. XII, 1974.
— Vol. XIV, 1976.
— Vol. XVII, 1981.
— Vol. XXI, 1988.
— *Foundations of Christian Faith* (Darton, Longman Todd, London, 1978).
Schillebeeckx, E., *Christ the Sacrament of the Encounter with God* (Sheed and Ward, London, 1963).
— *Revelation and Theology*, 2 vols. (Sheed and Ward, London, 1967).
— *World and Church* (Sheed and Ward, London, 1971).
— *Jesus. An Experiment in Christology* (Collins, London, 1979).
— *Christ. The Christian Experience in the Modern World* (SCM, London, 1980).
Shorter, A., *Theology of Mission* (Mercier Press, Cork, 1972).
— *Revelation and Its Interpretation* (Chapman, London, 1983).
Sobrino, J., *Christology at the Crossroads* (SCM, London, 1978).
Thiemann, R. F., *Revelation and Theology. The Gospel as Narrated Promise (University of Notre Dame Press, Notre Dame, Indiana, 1985).*
Thomas, O. C., *Attitudes Towards Other Religions* (SCM, London, 1969).
Thomas, M. M., *Risking Christ for Christ's Sake* (WCC, Geneva, 1987).
Tillich, P., *Christianity and the Encounter of the World Religions* (Columbia University Press, New York and London, 1963).
Troeltsch, E., *The Absoluteness of Christianity* (SCM, London, 1972) (Original German edition, 1929).
Urs von Balthasar, H., *A Theology of History* (Sheed and Ward, London, 1964).
— *Love alone the Way of Revelation* (Sheed and Ward, London, 1968).
— *Elucidations* (SPCK, London, 1975).

ARTICLES

Acharuparambil, D., "Hindu Salvation: a Human Conquest or a Divine Gift?", in *La Salvezza Oggi* (Acts of the Fifth International Congress of Missiology, Pontifical Urban University, Rome, 5-8 October 1988), pp. 227–240.
Anastasios, Bishop, "Emerging Perspectives on the Relationships of Christians to People of Other Faiths", in *International Review of Mission*, Vol. LXXXIII, No. 307, July 1988, pp. 332–346.
Borovoy, V., "What is Salvation? An Orthodox Statement", in *International Review of Mission*, Vol. LVII, No. 228, October 1968, pp. 209–241.
Bürkle, H., "Der christliche Anspruch angesichts der Welt-religionen heute", in *Absolutheit des Christentums* (ed. Kasper, W., Quaestiones Disputatae: Herder, Freiburg-in-Breisgau, 1977), pp. 83–103.
Chandran, J. R., "A Christian Approach to Other Religions", in *Bangalore Theological Forum*, Vol. VII/2, 1975, pp. 120ff.
Cobb, J., "Is Christianity a Religion?", in *Concilium*, June 1980, pp. 3–11.
Comblin, J., "The Current Debate on Christian Universality", in *Concilium*, May 1980, pp. 70–78.
Cote, R., "Some Pretensions to the Absolute in the History of Christian Missions", in *Concilium*, May 1980, pp. 14–22.

Daniélou, J., "La place des religieux dans la structure de l'Église", in G. Bauaúna (ed.) *L'Église de Vatican II*, Tome III, (Cerf, Paris, 1967) pp. 1173–1180.

Dhavamony, M., "Self-Understanding of World Religions as Religion", in *Gregorianum* 54/1, Pontificia Universitas Gregoriana, Rome, 1973, pp. 91–127.

— "Today's Challenge: Salvation Offered by Non-Christian Religions", in *La Salvezza Oggi*, pp. 81–100.

Di Noia, J. A., "Implicit Faith, General Revelation and the State of Non-Christians", in *The Thomist*, Vol. 47/2, April 1983, pp. 209–241.

D'Souza, P., "Iglesia, Misión y Reino de Dios en el contexto del Tercer Mundo", in *Misiones Extranjeras*, Vol. 68, 1982, pp. 93–116.

Dupré, W., "Ethnocentrism and the Challenge of Cultural Relativity", in *Concilium*, May 1980, pp. 3–13.

Dupuis, J. "The Salvific Value of Non-Christian Religions", in Dhavamony, M. (ed.) *Evangelization, Dialogue and Development* (Documenta Missionalia 5: Gregoriana, Rome, 1972) pp. 169–193.

Duquoc, C., "Christianity and its Claim to Universality", in *Concilium*, May 1980, pp. 59–69.

Esquerda Bifet, J., "El camino de la contemplación cristiana y no cristiana, camino diferenciado de salvación", in *La Salvezza Oggi*, pp. 345–360.

Fonner, M. G. "Christology: The Central Issue in Christian Theologies of Religions", in *Asian Journal of Theology*, Vol. 2/2, October 1988, pp. 327–341.

Gomes, A., "Theology of Non-Christian Religions", in *Euntes Docete*, Vol. XXIV, Rome 1971, pp. 372–391.

Hebblethwaite, P., "The Status of 'Anonymous Christians' ", in *The Heythrop Journal*, Vol. XVIII/1, January 1977, pp. 47–55.

Hogg, W. R., "Vatican II's *Ad Gentes*: A Twenty-Year Retrospective", in *International Bulletin of Missionary Research*, Vol. 9/4, October 1985, pp. 146–154.

Kalilombe, P. A., "The Salvific Value of African Religions", in *Christianisme et identité Africaines* (Actes du Premier Congrés des Biblistes Africains, Kinshasa 1980), pp. 205–219.

Kasper, W., "Are Non-Christian Religions Salvific?", in *Evangelization, Dialogue and Development*, pp. 157–168.

— "Die Kirche als universales Sakrament des Heils", in *Universales Christentum angesichts einer pluralen Welt*, (Bsteh, A., (ed.), Verlag St Gabriel, Mödling, 1976), pp. 33–55.

— "Offenbarung und Geheimnis vom christlichen Gottesverständnis", in *Sein als Offenbarung in Christentum und Hinduismus* (Bsteh, A., (ed.), Verlag St Gabriel, Mödling, 1984), pp. 219–232.

— "Die soteriologische Rolle der Kirche und die Sakramente des Heils", in *La Salvezza Oggi*, pp. 33–60.

Klaes, N., "Absolutheitsanspruch und Universalität des christlichen Glaubens — Probleme der Kirche in Indien", in *Zeitschrift für Mission*, XII (1986) pp. 22–33.

Knitter, P., "Christianity as Religion: True and Absolute?", in *Concilium*, June 1980, pp. 12–21.

— "Catholic Theology of Religions at a Crossroads", in *Concilium*, February 1986, pp. 99–107.

Küng, H., "Introduction: The Debate on the Word 'Religion' ", in *Concilium*, February 1986, pp. xi–xv.

— "Towards an Ecumenical Theology of Religions: Some Theses for Clarification", in *Concilium*, February 1986, pp. 119–125.

Lourdusamy, S. D., "Meeting of Religions, I: Indian Orientations", in *Meeting of Religions. New Orientations and Perspectives*, (Aykara, T. A., (ed.), Dharmaram Publications, Bangalore, 1978).

Martelet, G., "The Church as Sacrament", in *Theology Digest*, Vol. 22/1, Spring 1974, pp. 62–68.

McNamara, K., "Is There a Non-Christian Revelation?" in *Evangelization, Dialogue and Development*, pp. 147–155.

Pieris, A., "Non-Christian Religions and Cultures in Third World Theology", in *Vidyajyoti*, April 1982, pp. 158–170, and May-June 1982, pp. 227–245.

Pierson, P.E., "Roman Catholic Missions since Vatican II: An Evangelical Assessment", in *International Bulletin of Missionary Research*, Vol. 9/4, October 1985, pp. 165–167.

Piryns, E. D., "Current Roman Catholic Views of Other Religions", in *The Japan Missionary Bulletin*, XXXIX/2, Summer 1985, pp. 34–39.

Planells Almerich, J., "Inculturación, Un Reto Permanente" in *Misiones Extranjeras*, No. 104, March/April 1988, pp. 79–159.

Puthiadam, I., "Christian Faith and Life in a World of Religious Pluralism", in *Concilium*, May 1980, pp. 99–112.

Rahner, K., "Der Eine Jesus Christus und die Universalität des Heils", in *Universales Christentum angesichts einer pluralen Welt*, pp. 57–85.

— "Welt in Gott. Zum christlichen Schopfungsbegriff", in *Sein als Offenbarung in Christentum und Hinduismus*, pp. 69–82.

Rosato, P. J., "The Mission of the Spirit Within and Beyond the Church", in *The Ecumenical Review*, Vol. 41/3, July 1989, pp. 388–397.

Samartha, S. J., "Mission in a Religiously Plural World. Looking Beyond Tambaram 1938", in *International Review of Mission*, Vol. LXXXIII, No. 307, July 1988, pp. 311–324.

— "The Kingdom of God in a Religiously Plural World", in *The Ecumenical Review*, Vol. 32, No. 2 (1980), pp. 152–165.

Schineller, J. P. "Christ and the Church: A Spectrum of Views", in *Theological Studies*, Vol. 37 (1976), pp. 545–566.

Schreiter, R. J., "The Anonymous Christian and Christology", in *Missiology*, Vol. VI/1, January 1978, pp. 29–52.

Sharpe, E. J., "The Spirit and the Religions", in (Beyerhaus P. and Hallencretz C., (eds), *The Church Crossing Frontiers*, Studia Missionalia Upsaliensia, XI, Vanden-Hoech and Ruprecht, Gleerup).

Smith, W. C. "Mission, Dialogue and God's Will For Us", in *International Review of Mission*, Vol. LXXXIII, No. 307, July 1988, pp. 360–374.

Smulders, P., "L'Église sacrement du salut", in *L'Église de Vatican II*, pp. 313–338.

Stransky, T. F., "The Church and Other Religions", in International Bulletin of Missionary Research, October 1985, pp. 154–158.

Tan, W., "Religious Pluralism Revisited", in *Asian Journal of Theology*, Vol. 2/2, October 1988, pp. 342–349.

Tomko, Card. J., "Sfide Missionarie alla teologia della salvezza", in *La Salvezza Oggi*, pp. 13–32.

Wieser, T., "Report on the Salvation Study", in *International Review of Mission*, LVII, No. 228, October 1968, pp. 170–179.

Willems, B., "Who Belongs to the Church?", in *Concilium*, Vol. 1/1, January 1965, pp. 62–71.

Zoghby, E., "Unité et diversité de l'Église", in *L'Église de Vatican II*, pp. 493–516.